TEACHING 3-8

Related titles:
Asher Cashdan and Lyn Overall (eds): *Teaching in Primary Schools*
Janet Kay: *Protecting Children*
Andrew Pollard: *Reflective Teaching in the Primary School:
A Handbook for the Classroom* (*3rd edition*)
Andrew Pollard: *Readings for Reflective Teaching in the
Primary School*
Carole Sharman, Wendy Cross and Diana Vennis: *Observing
Children* (*2nd edition*)

Teaching 3–8

MEETING THE STANDARDS FOR INITIAL TEACHER TRAINING AND INDUCTION

Mark O'Hara

CONTINUUM
London and New York

Continuum

Wellington House 370 Lexington Avenue
125 Strand New York
London WC2R 0BB NY 10017–6503

First published 2000

British Library Cataloguing-in-Publication Data

A catalogue record for this book is available from the British Library.

ISBN 0–8264-4843-7

Designed and typeset by Ben Cracknell Studios

Printed and bound in Great Britain by Redwood Books, Trowbridge, Wilts

Contents

1 Knowledge and understanding   1

2 Planning, Teaching and Class Management   52

3 Monitoring, Assessment, Recording, Reporting and Accountability   100

4 Other Professional Requirements   130

Acknowledgements

I would like to thank colleagues at Sheffield Hallam University for their advice and suggestions in compiling this book, in particular Jackie Marsh and Graham Peacock. I would also like to thank friends and former colleagues, currently working at Carlton Park Nursery Infant School and St Bede's RC N/I/J School, for contributing some of the examples and documentation which illustrate the text.

Preface

This book is aimed at teacher training students on 3–8 courses, and newly qualified teachers working with the same age range. This age range is a crucial time in children's development, and effective teaching in nursery and lower primary education will help to lay the foundations for their future success both as learners and as citizens.

Good teaching is a complex, highly skilled activity requiring judgements on how to act. Becoming effective as a teacher will depend upon the acquisition of skills and knowledge through personal experience, the support and training received from other professionals, making reference to the literature on the subject and developing a good understanding of how young children learn. One of the devices by which initial teacher training (ITT) students are required to develop a positive and proactive approach to their own professional development is to demonstrate achievement against the Standards, or competences, set out in the Requirements for Courses of Initial Teacher Training and to use them to compile a Career Entry Profile (CEP). Once in post, newly qualified teachers (NQTs) are also required to address a further set of competences in order to complete their induction year successfully. This book uses competences contained in Annex A, Sections A–D of Circular 4/98 as the basis for discussing key aspects of 3–8 teaching and for directing trainee and newly qualified teachers towards further reading and sources of information.

Competences can
- provide clear goals and targets to aim for;
- engender greater confidence in trainees about the skills and knowledge that they have already acquired;
- help to establish exactly what areas should be covered by those training to become teachers; and
- give (future) employers some assurance about what an NQT can do.

However, competence approaches to teaching and teacher training are not without their shortcomings:

- It is possible for some competence statements to mean different things to different readers;
- competence statements tend to emphasize outcomes – they are statements about what

teachers must achieve; they do not in themselves always provide any insights into the process or processes by which these achievements are to be attained, nor can they necessarily guarantee that a competence, once demonstrated, will be demonstrated again at other times and in other contexts.

- Teaching is not just about acquiring skills and knowledge; it is also about the values and attitudes that impact upon a teacher's decision-making processes, values which are not always fully identified in a competency approach to training.

Teaching involves much more than the unthinking mastery of a set of competences. Teachers need to have lively intellects and be able to exercise understanding and judgement. They have to be adept at problem-solving and communication, and be able to make links and connections between theory and practice. Good teachers are thoughtful, creative, self-critical and believe that all children can make progress. Teachers need to be reflective in their practice and engage in self-appraisal, reading and research, rather than simply ticking off a list of competences.

One of the difficulties facing a writer of an introductory text on 3–8 teaching is the temptation to try to cover every aspect in depth. This is clearly impossible in the space available. Consequently, this book offers an introduction to some of the issues and ideas relating to the Standards in Circular 4/98, and directs the reader to further sources of information. It aims to provide a platform from which trainees and NQTs can launch themselves into the further research and investigation that will be necessary if they are either to achieve qualified teacher status (QTS), or complete successfully their induction period in nurseries or in schools.

How to Use the Book

Each of the chapters begins with a brief summary outlining those aspects of the Standards for the Award of Qualified Teacher Status that are touched upon. Although the chapters utilize the broad headings found in Circular 4/98 some of the individual statements have been located in other chapters to avoid duplication.

SUMMARY

This chapter deals with the knowledge and understanding expected of trainee and newly qualified 3–8 teachers. It will provide you with an overview of the structure and scope of the 3–8 curriculum. The chapter will also consider some of the theories concerning young children's development, in particular their intellectual development, and the impact this has on teaching and learning. Finally, the chapter examines some of the detail of the 3–8 curriculum using the Early Learning Goals as a framework and investigates how National Curriculum subjects can arise out of these areas of learning.

By the end of the chapter you should

- have an overview of the National Curriculum programmes of study and level descriptions as well as knowledge of SCAA's 'Desirable Outcomes for Children's Learning on Entering Compulsory Education' (A2di, A3a).

Within each chapter each section begins with a brief audit statement linking the contents more closely to the Standards.

By the end of this section you should

• be familiar with ways of establishing safe environments for 3–8 pupils which support their learning and in which they feel secure and confident (B4j).

X

At various points throughout the text, Example boxes indicate the use of exemplar material linked to the topic under discussion. All the names of pupils, teachers, nurseries and schools have been altered or deleted to maintain anonymity.

Gentle steering of a discussion

A class of Y1 children were listening and responding to questions about a story that their teacher was reading. The teacher asked the children what they thought was about to happen. Ellen put up her hand and the teacher said, 'Yes Ellen. What do you think will happen?' Ellen responded, 'I went to my Gran's on Saturday.' The teacher replied, 'Did you? That's very interesting. Do you think you could tell us a bit more about it when we've finished our story? Thank you. Now then, can anyone tell us what they think is going to happen next?'

At other points there are suggestions boxes on how trainee and newly qualified teachers can begin to address the competences set out in the Standards

Running circle time activities with infants

• Do not make the group too large with younger infants, and do not make the task too complicated.
• Remember the age and maturity of the children. Having to sit still and passively for long periods is likely to provoke disruption and undermine the purposes of the activity.
• 'Little and often' can be a useful motto for those working with younger pupils. These children are likely to benefit from more frequent, shorter sessions that encourage greater participation.
• Simple rules and conventions can be introduced to help get circle time activities up and running with the minimum of fuss, for example developing special signs and signals for gaining children's attention, or passing an object round the group which confers the right to speak on the holder.

Each chapter also contains suggestions on further reading and sources of information that trainee and newly qualified teachers can use to enhance and extend their knowledge and understanding.

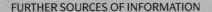

FURTHER SOURCES OF INFORMATION

Browne, A. (1996) *Developing Language and Literacy 3–8*. London: Chapman.

Marsh, J. and Hallet, E. (eds) (1999) *Desirable Literacies: Approaches to Language and Literacy in the Early Years*. London: Chapman.

Whitehead, M. (1997) *Language and Literacy in the Early Years*. Buckingham: Open University Press.

Introduction

The Requirements for Courses of Initial Teacher Training (DfEE, 1998a) contain both general statements and additional statements relating to 3–8 education. As well as the additional Standards aimed at 3–8 trainees in Annex A, there are also sections of Annexes B, D and E which need to be considered from the 3–8 perspective, as well as important issues relating to early literacy. Consequently, some sections in the book deal specifically with 3–5 provision in line with these national Standards (DfEE, 1998).

Chapter 1 deals with knowledge and understanding of the 3–8 curriculum. The chapter uses the broad areas of learning from the Early Learning Goals as a framework within which to discuss the breadth of the 3–8 curriculum. Student teachers and NQTs need to

- be familiar with the overall structure of the Desirable Outcomes / Early Learning Goals and the National Curriculum;
- be aware of the content of the various subjects and areas of learning; and
- be familiar with ways in which young children learn.

Chapter 2 covers planning, teaching and class management. Knowing *how* to teach something effectively to young children is every bit as important as knowing *what* to teach. Teachers of 3–8 pupils need to

- be able to plan and deliver the curriculum;
- be able to take into account the needs and abilities of pupils, including pupils with Special Educational Needs (SEN);
- be highly efficient organizers and managers of the learning environment; and
- hone their skills in working with and leading teams of professional colleagues.

Chapter 3 addresses the increasingly important area of assessment, recording and reporting. Assessing children's progress and recording the results plays a crucial part in the planning–teaching cycle. Similarly, teachers are becoming increasingly accountable to parents and society at large. Their effectiveness is constantly monitored and their results reported.

Chapter 4 deals with the other professional requirements to which all teachers, including 3–8 teachers, are subject. Teachers have to conduct themselves within an environment governed by extensive regulation, laws and systems. Trainee and newly qualified members of the profession need to

- have a working knowledge of the legislation relating to equality of opportunity, health and safety, and children's welfare;
- fulfil their responsibility to maintain good order in the classroom, without which there can be no successful teaching;
- be effective at establishing partnerships with parents;
- have an understanding of how schools and nurseries are managed;
- engage in whole-school and team approaches to delivering the complete curriculum; and
- be aware of their responsibility for their own continuing professional development.

1

Knowledge and Understanding

SUMMARY

This chapter deals with the knowledge and understanding expected of trainee and newly qualified 3–8 teachers. It will provide you with an overview of the structure and scope of the 3–8 curriculum. The chapter will also consider some of the theories concerning young children's development, in particular their intellectual development, and the impact such theories have on teaching and learning. Finally, the chapter examines some of the detail of the 3–8 curriculum using the Early Learning Goals as a framework and examining how National Curriculum subjects can arise out of these areas of learning.

By the end of this chapter you should

- have an overview of the National Curriculum programmes of study and level descriptions as well as knowledge of SCAA's 'Desirable Outcomes for Children's Learning on Entering Compulsory Education' (A2di, A3a).

Understanding the 3–8 Curriculum

By the end of this section you should

- understand the purposes, scope, structure and balance of the National Curriculum Orders in the primary phase (A2a);
- have an overview of the breadth of content covered by the pupils' National Curriculum across the primary core and foundation subjects and RE (A2b);
- begin to understand the progression from the 'Desirable Outcomes for Children's Learning on Entering Compulsory Education' to KS1, and the progression from KS1 to KS2 (A2div).

The Curriculum for Nursery and Reception Pupils

High-quality under-5s education can do much to lay the foundations for children's future successes in learning, but the rationale behind such provision concerns more than just preparation for future educational experiences. Education of the under-5s is part of a continuum beginning in the home and moving on to compulsory schooling. The broad aims for under-5 education are very similar to those for the over-5s, with an additional emphasis on the considerable amount of care that very young children require, care which is intrinsically linked to their education (DfEE, 1990).

The structure, organization and delivery of the curriculum in nurseries is often different to that in primary schools and ought to be viewed as the best way of addressing the particular needs of 3–5-year-olds during this crucial period of their development (QCA, 1998b). The education of 3- to 5-year-old children should be recognized as a distinctive stage in the continuum of learning and be valued in its own right. The 1990 Report to the Committee of Inquiry into the Quality of the Educational Experience offered to 3- and 4-year-olds 'Starting with Quality', proposed an under-5s curriculum with content based around broad areas of experience and learning rather than subject headings. The publication of *Desirable Outcomes for Children's Learning* (SCAA, 1996) reduced the broad areas of experience and learning from nine to six, and these areas were retained in the Early Learning Goals (QCA/DfEE, 1999). The decision to view the curriculum in these terms was based on the Committee's understanding of the characteristics and needs of young children, a desire to ensure breadth and balance, and a wish to achieve continuity with the National Curriculum.

1990 areas of experience	1996 Desirable Outcomes and 1999 Early Learning Goals
linguistic	
aesthetic and creative	
human and social	personal and social development
mathematical	language and literacy
moral	mathematics
physical	knowledge and understanding of the world
scientific	physical development
technological	creative development
spiritual (DfEE, 1990)	(SCAA, 1996; QCA/DfEE, 1999)

3

In 1999 the Qualifications and Curriculum Authority (QCA) led the process of reviewing the Desirable Learning Outcomes. The consultation document proposed

- the replacement of the Desirable Learning Outcomes with Early Learning Goals;
- the establishment of a foundation stage of education for 3- to 5-year-old pupils in nursery and reception classes; and
- the production of curriculum guidance materials including exemplar material for nursery and reception practitioners.

Although the QCA documentation retains the same areas of learning as those contained in the SCAA documentation (1996), the Early Learning Goals, are more precise. They represent what most children will be expected to achieve by the end of their time in reception classes. In addition, the establishment of a foundation stage alongside these more precise learning goals is intended to result in a smoother transition for children encountering the National Curriculum at Year 1.

Example of Desirable Outcomes and Early Learning Goals

Creative development
These outcomes focus on the development of children's imagination and their ability to communicate and to express ideas and feelings in creative ways (SCAA, 1996, p.4).

Examples of proposed Early Learning Goals
By the end of the reception year, most children will
- be confident to try new activities, initiate ideas and speak in a familiar group;
- be able to maintain attention, concentrate and sit quietly when appropriate; and
- be interested, excited and motivated to learn.   (QCA, 1999, p.23)

The National Curriculum for Key Stages 1 and 2

The Education Reform Act of 1988 (ERA) placed a statutory responsibility upon schools to provide a curriculum that would

- promote the spiritual, moral, cultural, mental and physical development of pupils at the school and of society; and
- prepare pupils for the opportunities, responsibilities and experiences of adult life.

(NCC, 1990)

The establishment of these principles significantly influenced the subsequent scope and structure of the National Curriculum for primary schools. It meant that a broad and balanced curriculum should be offered to pupils at both Key Stage 1 (children 5–7 years of age) and Key Stage 2 (children 7–11 years of age). It also meant that this broad and balanced curriculum should be relevant to the needs of the pupils taking it. The curriculum outlined in the Act was comprised of

- the National Curriculum subjects;
- Religious Education for all children over 5; and
- a series of cross-curricular elements and additional subjects which together would form the whole curriculum.

National Curriculum subjects

The National Curriculum for Key Stages 1 and 2 has been subject to numerous refinements and modifications in the period since its introduction, for example the introduction in 1995 of a streamlined National Curriculum with more compact programmes of study to make it more manageable. However, the subjects themselves have remained largely constant.

Each subject in the National Curriculum has a set of **Programmes of Study** (PoS) for Key Stages 1 and 2, which are designed to help teachers plan the curriculum offered to children. Programmes of Study are designed to assist teachers in planning.

Each subject in the National Curriculum has a set of **Attainment Targets** (ATs), broken down into level descriptions, designed to help teachers make judgements about children's learning and achievements. Attainment Targets are designed to assist teachers in assessment.

Core subjects in the National Curriculum	Foundation subjects in the National Curriculum
English	Design and technology
Mathematics	Geography
Science	History
	Art
	Music
	Physical education

Information and communications technology (ICT) first appeared in the National Curriculum distributed amongst the various other subjects. During the revisions of 1995 it was subsequently brought together into what amounts to an additional subject in the documentation, with its own PoS and ATs, but retaining a high degree of relevance for most of the other subjects.

The introduction of the National Curriculum carried with it an inherent tension between the desire to offer pupils a broad and balanced curriculum and the desire to raise standards, particularly in subjects like English and mathematics. This tension has been further exacerbated by developments such as the introduction of targets for SATs results and of literacy and numeracy hours for pupils in Key Stages 1 and 2. The consequences of this initial tension (and subsequent developments) have included pressure on the amount of time available for delivering the foundation subjects necessary for a broad and balanced curriculum. Materials published by the Qualifications and Curriculum Authority (1998a), constituted a recognition of this pressure and were an attempt to retain the commitment to breadth and balance by developing more flexible approaches to the teaching of subjects other than English and mathematics.

The cross-curricular elements

The cross-curricular elements were originally envisaged as important areas of learning with relevance across the National Curriculum as a whole. They were not restricted to any one subject area – their purpose was to pull together the broad education of the individual and augment the basic curriculum as set out in the core and foundation subjects (NCC, 1990). These elements included cross-curricular themes, skills and dimensions.

Cross-curricular themes offer opportunities for discussion of values and beliefs as well as adding to children's knowledge and understanding. They include

- Economic and Industrial Understanding
- Careers Education and Guidance
- Health Education
- Education for Citizenship
- Environmental Education.

(NCC, 1990)

Cross-curricular skills are those skills that are relevant (in varying degrees) to all subjects but which are not the preserve of any one subject. They include

- study skills;
- problem-solving skills;
- communication skills;
- numeracy skills;
- ICT skills; and
- personal and social skills. (NCC, 1990)

Cross-curricular dimensions are closely associated with the principles of entitlement arising from the 1988 Education Reform Act. They concern the ethos and philosophy of education and are designed to promote equality and fairness. The cross-curricular dimensions include

- preparation for life in a multi-cultural society;
- access (to the curriculum) for children with different learning abilities; and
- equality of opportunity for all. (NCC, 1990)

Since their appearance in National Curriculum Council (NCC) documentation (1990) some of these cross-curricular elements (particularly numeracy, the literacy strand of communication and ICT) have assumed increasing prominence in education. Others, however, have retained a status that is at best imprecise, with, in some cases, little attention being paid to them. Teachers, understandably, prioritize those statutory subjects such as English and mathematics where public accountability is greatest.

Understanding how young children learn

By the end of this section you should

- have developed some understanding of how pupils' learning is affected by their intellectual, emotional and social development (A2c);
- know about some of the ideas that young children can hold and some of the misconceptions and mistakes that they can make (A2dvi);
- understand the importance of first-hand experience, cooperation, play and talk as vehicles for young children's learning (B5g).

The Work of the Interactionists

Various schools of thought have emerged which attempt to understand and explain children's development, and this section deals with the work of psychologists and researchers such as Piaget, Athey, Bruner and Vygotsky. The work of these interactionists and social interactionists (Bruce, 1997) has had a significant impact upon current practice in 3–8 settings and is characterized by the idea that children learn best when they are interacting with their environment, with their peers and with adults.

Jean Piaget

The Swiss psychologist Jean Piaget made a major and ground breaking contribution to our understanding of how children think and learn. Through his research he hoped to understand and explain how young children come to make sense of the world around them and to develop ways of operating effectively in it. As a result of his observations and experiments he postulated a series of developmental stages which children went through in regular and ordered sequence. In each of these stages the children were refining their thinking in the light of experience. The sequence was invariable, children could not bypass stages or make short cuts to reach more advanced stages. Nor was progression from one stage to the next envisaged by Piaget as a revolutionary, overnight affair, but was instead an evolutionary and more gradual process. He included guidance on the ages at which children go through these stages (see below) although he acknowledged that these were only an approximation and believed that while children were travelling the same route they were not necessarily progressing at the same speed.

Piaget's stages

1. **Sensorimotor**. Children are getting to know the world in terms of physical actions that they can perform. (Age 0–2 years)
2. **Pre-operational**. Children have not yet acquired fully logical thinking. (Age 2–7 years)
3. **Concrete operational**. Children can think logically about problems that are concrete i.e. here and now. (Age 7–12 years)
4. **Formal operational**. Children are able to think rationally about abstract or hypothetical problems. (Age 12 onwards)

A key element in Piaget's theories was the idea that children are not passive learners soaking up the wisdom of adults. Instead, for Piaget, children were actively constructing meaning and ideas about how the world works. He used the concepts of assimilation, disequilibrium and accommodation to explain the process of learning.

A child would *assimilate* knowledge as a result of first-hand experience.

Subsequent experience would force the child to reevaluate his/her original ideas in the light of new situations and observations in order to *accommodate* to the new reality.

The lack of equilibrium or *disequilibrium* caused by encountering a situation which did not conform to the child's old model (*schema*) of the world was resolved as the child incorporated the new knowledge and experience into his/her existing mental models, thus improving and enhancing them.

For Piaget, progression in intellectual development was the result of the loss, and subsequent restoration at a new higher level, of equilibrium. In Piaget's model, the older and more mature the children, the more adept they are at taking into account increasing quantities of information and exploring increasingly complex strategies to help them solve problems and operate effectively in their environment.

Finally, although the idea did not originate with Piaget, a controversial element in his theories was the notion of readiness. If a child found a problem too difficult then this constituted evidence that the child was not yet ready to learn. In other words, the child's mental schemas had not yet reached a level where restructuring was possible.

Chris Athey and schema

Piaget's work on schema has been subsequently refined and expanded by researchers such as Chris Athey and Cathy Nutbrown. Athey (1990) and others have observed that, as children make sense of the world through interacting with it, some of them appear to exhibit patterns of repeatable behaviour. Through her research Athey was able to identify a number of different schemas.

Evidence of schemas

A young child is observed running in circles during outdoor play.
During painting activities the same child likes to paint circles regularly.
The child appears fascinated by artefacts and objects that are circular in shape.
This child may be showing evidence of a schema. She/he appears to be establishing connections in relation to circles.

Athey's work suggested four ways in which schema might manifest themselves.

1. through motor actions (i.e. physical movement);
2. through symbolic functioning (i.e. representing something through drawings or letters);
3. through functional dependency relationships (i.e. 'I've done x so that y can happen');
4. through thought.

Athey's, and subsequent, research has suggested that not all children show evidence of exploring schemas, and those that do, do not necessarily follow a set pattern. Furthermore, some children may explore more than one schema at a time. That said, Athey's work on the concept of schema is very useful in understanding how some young children learn, and can help to make sense of nursery/classroom observations of young children's actions.

Jerome Bruner and Lev Vygotsky

Like Piaget, Athey and others, Jerome Bruner has made an important contribution to understanding cognitive development in children. By using Piaget's ideas and linking these to his own theories Bruner too developed a stage model. He was particularly interested in the part played by experience in cognitive development, concluding that careful instruction (guiding a child to new ways of coping with a new problem) could aid the process of maturation.

Bruner's stages
1. **Enactive stage**: understanding through first hand experience;
2. **Iconic stage**: understanding through images;
3. **Symbolic stage**: children able to express ideas through words and numbers and have acquired the concept of conservation.

Bruner's research suggested that children were capable of intellectual achievements (at an earlier point than that predicted by Piaget) as a result of instruction and carefully structured environments. This challenged Piaget's idea of readiness. For Bruner, passively waiting for children to become ready to learn might necessitate a very long delay indeed. As a result, the concept of readiness could actually lead to a lowering of educational standards and teacher expectations. While teachers of young children do need to be sensitive to a child's needs, abilities and development, they also need to be prepared to intervene – questioning, guiding and instructing in an effort to extend and challenge thinking. In Bruner's model, facilitating pupils' progress through the use of appropriate support materials and intervention would provide children with scaffolding upon which they could construct increasingly advanced ways of thinking and understanding the world.

Bruner also made two further contributions to our understanding of children's development which have had a powerful influence on 3–8 teaching. Firstly, he suggested that there was a social dimension to cognitive development, whereby a child's learning is also influenced and affected by those experiences involving interaction with others, both children and adults. Communication and language therefore played a crucial role in learning and cognitive development. Secondly, Bruner advocated a spiral curriculum for children in which they would revisit topics at regular intervals thus advancing their learning towards higher levels of understanding.

Knowledge and understanding of the world

Desirable Outcomes

10

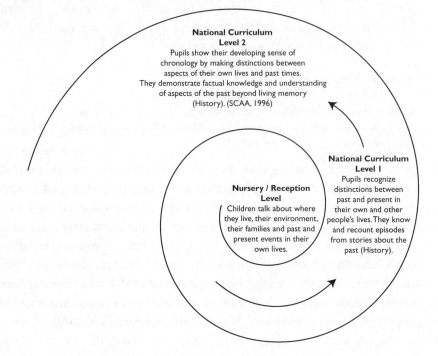

**National Curriculum
Level 2**
Pupils show their developing sense of
chronology by making distinctions between
aspects of their own lives and past times.
They demonstrate factual knowledge and understanding
of aspects of the past beyond living memory
(History). (SCAA, 1996)

**National Curriculum
Level 1**
Pupils recognize
distinctions between
past and present in
their own and other
people's lives. They know
and recount episodes
from stories about the
past (History).

**Nursery / Reception
Level**
Children talk about where
they live, their environment,
their families and past and
present events in their
own lives.

Vygotsky too, recognized the importance of communication and language in cognitive
development. He also advocated the use of scaffolding to advance children's learning and
developed the notion of a 'zone of proximal development' (ZPD) to explain his ideas.

what someone (a child) can do unaided	**zone of proximal development**	what someone (a child) can achieve with help from someone more skilful/knowledgeable

For those taking a Vygotskian perspective, readiness is not simply a question of a child's
existing knowledge or schemas, it is also influenced by a child's capacity to learn. The
implication of this idea is that teachers of young children need to make sound
assessments of pupils' progress and use these to gauge the amount of scaffolding
required to support learning. This idea will be pursued further in Chapter 2 in relation
to differentiation and Gardner's notion of multiple intelligences (Cotton, 1995).

The work of interactionists like Piaget, social interactionists such as Bruner and
Vygotsky, and later researchers such as Athey, can be seen informing current

practice in 3–8 settings. To begin with, young children are perceived as active learners who benefit from, and are thus provided with, relevant first-hand experience. Schools and nurseries assist pupils in making sense of the world by exploring objects, materials and feelings in meaningful situations. The children's natural curiosity is harnessed as they are encouraged to ask why and how things are as they are. Nurseries and schools also recognize that young children gain a great deal personally, socially and cognitively from interacting with others.

Playing and Talking

Building in opportunities for play and talk are essential features of teaching and learning in 3–8 settings. With young children, playing and talking are central to learning. Reception and nursery teachers recognize the fundamental importance of language development, both for the children's future adult prospects and their educational achievements. Oral language is the basis for literacy, and as a result teachers give significant consideration both to the quantity and quality of talk. At the same time, the need for play opportunities has long been seen as an essential part of the learning process for these pupils. Young children learn well in situations that include an element of *doing*, and their teachers pay particular attention to the need to offer hands-on experiences including those of play. Play offers children the chance to learn in contexts in which they are highly receptive. It is much more than simply a recreational time-filler; it is a valuable approach to learning.

Types of play

Free play offers young children the chance to interact with their peers in activities that they themselves have devised and through which they can express themselves and explore things that are of special interest to them. Such play can be a powerful method of arousing and sustaining children's curiosity and motivation.

Exploratory play, for example involving sand or water, provides opportunities for children to be creative and to explore and improve their knowledge of the world around them.

Construction play gives children experience in working with a wide range of materials and opportunities to acquire practical skills.

Games and puzzles provide children with interesting situations in which they can hone their problem solving skills, cooperate with others, and learn to compete in non-aggressive ways. Increasingly, many games and simulations are available using ICT. Although some schools and nurseries remain to be convinced of the educational worth of such games, it is possible that they may offer children the chance to practise physical skills such as hand-eye coordination; to develop their intellectual potential, demanding memory and planning; and promote social and emotional development by encouraging children to share, take turns, cooperate, negotiate and make decisions for themselves.

Role play and imaginary play are very effective in providing young children with opportunities to be creative and resourceful. They offer children the chance to lear meaningful contexts and to express their feelings verbally as well as practising and reinforcing social skills (Abbott, 1994). Starting from *recreating* the children's own experiences (shopping or visiting a café), role-play areas can proceed to offer pupils the chance to *create*, and be part of, new and imaginative scenarios (a jungle camp or a fairy story such as 'Jack and the Beanstalk'). Such play enables young children to practise and learn new or unfamiliar ways of using language, and to come to terms with real-life situations that they might find worrying (for example, going to the dentist). Where the role-play area is connected to themes or topics that are ongoing in the nursery/classroom, opportunities are created for children to practise and reinforce learning across the curriculum.

Getting the most out of role-play in 3–8 settings

- Take it seriously as a vehicle for learning. Plan for it, with clear educational objectives for a particular role-play setting.
- Be ready to become part of children's imaginary scenarios to help them practise skills, learn new ways of using language and ensure that the equality of opportunity offered in the rest of the curriculum is also offered in socio-dramatic play.
- Enhance the quality of play by ensuring that the role-play area contains plenty of stimulating equipment and materials. Where possible, real-life artefacts may be better than pretend ones for promoting responsible behaviour. Common artefacts for role-play include tables, chairs, beds, a range of clothing (male, female, multicultural), accessories (purses/wallets, jewellery, hats) and kitchen artefacts (cooker, sink, washing machine).
- Use trips and visits to real locations (for example, shops and cafés) to provide children with ideas about ways of behaving and likely events in a given context.

Themes for role-play areas

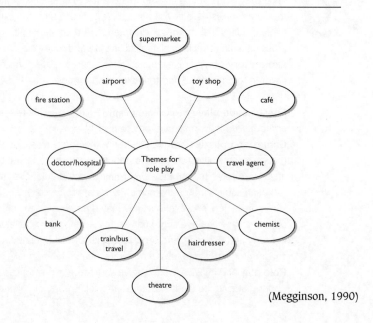

(Megginson, 1990)

12

While nurseries and many reception classes offer a wide range of play activities for pupils, the choice often narrows as children move through the infant school and into Y3, frequently becoming restricted to work with construction kits and computer simulations. In addition, an increasingly large distinction is sometimes drawn between playing and working as children get older. Not only does the range of play activities become narrower, but some teachers seem much less willing to allocate time to play. Rather than being seen as an approach to learning, play sometimes appears to be regarded as a luxury that actually takes time away from that pursuit. Although this is not surprising given the emphasis on literacy and numeracy, meeting government-set targets for SATs results and ever-increasing levels of teacher accountability, it is still a great shame as play offers a wide range of potential learning opportunities.

Developing play and talk in 3–8 settings

- Stimulate children's imagination through the experiences offered.
- Provide space, resources and time for pretend play.
- Build learning opportunities from across the curriculum into those play activities taking place.
- Be ready to become active participants in children's play from time-to-time (scaffolding). While it is important not to let involvement become interference, teachers may well have to get drawn into play situations if they wish their learning objectives to be realized.
- Offer opportunities for children to extend and improve their oral language skills through working in pairs and groups and by providing a wide range of shared experiences.
- Think aloud with pupils, providing opportunities for reasoning, investigating and solving simple problems verbally.
- Encourage children to question and share their ideas.
- Use bilingual teachers and support staff to facilitate the play and talk of pupils with English as a second language or special educational needs (SEN).
- Use activities rooted in the wider curriculum, such as art and music to develop children's communication and literacy skills.
- Provide access to adults, as older people can provide very useful models of how to use language appropriately, how to listen, and how to respond. For example, listening to stories can be a powerful way to introduce new words, extend the children's experience of language and help them to become more familiar with the rhythms, patterns and structures of language. Such adult–pupil contacts can also be important in developing other strands of literacy; for example, young children often get some of their earliest ideas about reading and writing from watching and copying the adults around them whom they see reading and writing themselves.

Pupil ideas, Misconceptions and Errors

The work of psychologists such as Piaget and others has been influential in suggesting how children develop their understanding of language, number and the world around them over time. The Standards contained in Circular 4/98 however, refer to pupil mistakes and misconceptions (A2dvi). Annexes C and D highlight some of the most common errors in English and mathematics. Although the documentation is not quite as specific for science there is plenty of other literature on this topic and young children's incomplete scientific ideas are well documented in areas such as physical changes, electricity, force and energy, (Osborne and Freyberg, 1985; Selley, 1999). When responding to pupil 'mistakes and misconceptions', trainee and newly qualified 3–8 teachers need to appreciate that a child's mistake or misconception may actually constitute partial understanding that can, and will, become more complete as they mature and gain in experience.

It is not possible in the space available to deal with the whole curriculum or go into minute detail as to how errors and misconceptions can be overcome and pupils' ideas and understanding enhanced. This section will therefore restrict itself to some general remarks on the subjects of English, mathematics and science.

Mistakes and misconceptions

In **English**, mistakes often arise from an incomplete understanding of grammatical rules, for example 'I weren't!' or 'Miss, we done it'. Children may also experience problems over spelling, make errors in reading and have difficulties with punctuation.

In **mathematics**, children may experience difficulties associated with counting on, have misunderstandings over place value, or be unclear over the order of subtraction. The use of the phrase *take away* when referring to subtraction is acceptable when young children can physically take away items such as sweets, bricks or marbles; however, they will also need a more extensive repertoire of terms including *from* and *subtract*. Some difficulties in mathematics can arise from the fact that there may be numerous ways of asking children to do the same thing:
• 'find the sum of 1 and 5'
• 'add 5 to 1'
• 'add 1 and 5'
• 'what number is 5 more than 1'?

In **science**, some pupil ideas and misconceptions can arise from the fact that, although the children are familiar with a particular word, they have only ever heard its everyday usage and are unaware that it also has a much more precise meaning. The concept of energy is one example. The following scientific ideas were encountered by 3–8 student teachers during an infant teaching practice:
• strawberries classified as animals
• big things sink, little things float
• big things are heavy, little things are light
• plants need to be put in a greenhouse, in the sun, in order to germinate and grow
• heavy objects fall faster than light objects because they are heavier
• seeds contain miniature plants
• a material is a fabric.

Young children can develop certain ideas, make errors and hold misconceptions for a variety of reasons. It is certainly the case that the language used can be at the root of some problems. In some cases teachers may be using vocabulary that is inappropriately advanced or strange to the children. In other cases children may confuse similar-sounding words. However, not all errors arise from language difficulties and some problems can also occur when children draw incomplete conclusions from their first-hand experiences and observations.

Error or misconception?

A group of reception children had been exploring whether a range of objects would float or sink when immersed in the water tray. Their teacher joined them and asked them to suggest how they could tell whether an object would be a floater or a sinker. The children replied that 'red things sink and the other colours float'. When the teacher looked at the objects tested she realized that in this particular instance that was indeed the case.

Having identified pupil ideas, errors and misconceptions, and having made some judgements concerning possible causes, teachers are then faced with the question of what to do about them.

Responding to pupil ideas, misconceptions and errors

- Allow for the age and maturity of the child. What might consitute an error for an 8-year-old might be a reasonable level of understanding for a reception child.
- Respond in supportive and helpful ways that promote progress and do not belittle and demotivate.
- Children can learn a lot from mistakes if they are handled in a sensitive way and are accompanied by regular experiences of success. Some sensitive correction can be instructive for children and may even be motivating as they feel more skilled and knowledgeable as a result.
- Picking up on every little error and correcting incessantly is likely to make children less confident and less willing to take risks and 'have a go'.
- Introduce activities and experiences that result in challenges to children's current understanding (causing disequilibrium) to encourage them to modify their ideas.
- Do not make the intellectual jump required of pupils so large that they are unable to link contrary experiences with their existing ideas.
- Remember that experience alone guarantees nothing. Be aware that some children may incorporate contrary experience into their existing schemas rather than alter the schema. Teachers need to intervene to help children develop their skills, knowledge and understanding (scaffolding). Using focused questions and making time to discuss children's experiences and ideas are useful ways of doing this.

The rest of the chapter uses the areas of learning set out in the *Desirable Outcomes for Children's Learning* (SCAA, 1996) and the Early Learning Goals (QCA/DfEE, 1999) to provide an overall structure into which comments on the subjects in the

National Curriculum for Key Stages 1 and 2 have been integrated. Although it has no corresponding heading in the Desirable Outcomes and Early Learning Goals, the final section on ICT reflects its increasing importance across the 3–8 age range.

Personal and Social Development

AUDIT

By the end of this section you should

- have increased your understanding of how pupils' learning is affected by their emotional and social development (A2c, B5bi, B5e);
- be aware of the purposes of RE in the primary curriculum (A2a-b).

This section deals with personal and social education for 3–8 pupils. It also includes reference to Religious Education for infant pupils as this is one of the subjects in which the over-5s can be encouraged to increase their skills and sensitivity at this stage of their development.

Nurseries and schools seek to help young children develop their understanding of social and personal values. In so doing, teachers of young children are often building on the work of the family, starting from and continuing the good work done by most parents and carers, and ameliorating the worst effects of the minority (DES, 1992). While most children can begin to develop self-confidence and an understanding of right and wrong through the support of their families, for some, their development in this area is impeded by stressful home circumstances which militate against success. Children whose self-image is poor, for example, may find working successfully as part of a group difficult.

Actively promoting children's personal and social development benefits teachers in 3–8 settings by encouraging good behaviour and achievement on the part of the pupils. At the same time, it provides the children with strategies for reconciling social and emotional conflicts and offers opportunities for them to establish good interpersonal relationships. These experiences will be of use to them during their continuing education and later as adults.

Promoting pupils' personal and social development

Aims	Strategies
1. Help children to develop an understanding of their position and role within their family context.	1. Encourage children to develop an awareness of their position in the family: • Naming family members. • Describing family roles and responsibilities. • Seek information and clarification about family members. • Develop family trees/maps.
2. Help children to become increasingly aware that they are part of a larger community.	2. Get children to learn about their community: • Elicit children's knowledge and understanding of where they live. • Ask children to identify and describe features of their neighbourhood. • Discuss community rules relating to road safety, littering, signs and symbols.
3. Encourage children to develop positive relationships outside the family context in nursery/school enabling them to participate as members of a group.	3. Teach children that cooperating, taking turns, waiting and becoming less egocentric are all valued behaviours. Encourage them to • help and look after others • take turns • line up and move sensibly as a group/class • listen to other children and adults • share with others • talk about fair and unfair behaviour • show consideration to others in the group • show respect for others in their class and in their surroundings.

4. Increase and extend children's self-awareness.	4. • Encourage children to take increasing responsibilities.
	• Help them to develop increasingly realistic expectations of themselves.
	• Offer opportunities for children to exercise increasing control over their own learning experiences, their environment and their resources.
	• Encourage them to
	  • dress themselves after dance/movement
	  • go to the toilet independently
	  • look after their possessions properly, e.g. hanging up their coats after outdoor play
	  • resolve disagreements amicably and independently
	  • express themselves confidently
	  • try new things and have a go
	  • tidy up after themselves
	  • tell the truth
	  • look for alternative/independent solutions to problems.

17

Circle Time

Circle time is one way of promoting self-esteem and fostering caring relationships in groups and classes of children. The highly structured nature of these activities (they often require children to adhere closely to certain rules and conventions) may make them less appropriate for some of the youngest (nursery) children, but with older children they can offer teachers interesting and fun ways of helping children to

- develop strategies for dealing positively with their feelings;
- cope with change;
- deal with conflict;
- solve problems; and
- develop tolerance towards their peers.

Circle time activities can help young children to acquire the sorts of social skills necessary to be able to live and work together in a more harmonious fashion and offer pupils the chance to experience

> being trusted; being respected; being successful; being praised; being listened to; listening to others; cooperating; working constructively in groups.
>
> (Curry and Bromfield, 1995)

An example of Circle time with Y2 children

Warm up activity
A group of twelve children and their teacher sit together on the carpet. The children are in a circle. There is a gap in the circle. The child on the right of the gap has to ask someone to come and sit next to them. (Rule: boys must pick a girl and girls must pick a boy.)

Introducing the theme
The teacher tells the children that they are going to be thinking about things that make them sad and what they can do to help other people who are sad. The teacher says 'I feel sad when . . .' The child on the right tells the group what makes them sad and so on around the circle. (Rule: everyone must start with the phrase 'I feel sad when . . .')

Main activity relating to theme
The teacher groups the children into threes and asks the children to think about what they could do if they see someone who is sad. The teacher spends time with each group, offering encouragement and sharing ideas.

Plenary
The children reform the original circle of twelve and the teacher chairs the feedback session in which children can report to the whole group on their ideas and suggestions. Children who are reluctant to comment in front of everyone else are not forced to do so.

Concluding activity
A short finishing-off activity offering praise and recognition to one or two children in the group, for example, giving someone a round of applause, patting them on the back.

Running circle time activities with infants

- Do not make the group too large with younger infants, and do not make the task too complicated.
- Remember the age and maturity of the children. Having to sit still and passively for long periods is likely to provoke considerable disruption and undermine the purposes of the activity.
- 'Little and often' can be a useful motto for those working with younger pupils. These children are likely to benefit from more frequent, shorter sessions that encourage greater participation.
- Simple rules and conventions can be introduced to help get circle time activities up and running with the minimum of fuss, for example developing special signs and signals for gaining children's attention, or passing an object round the group which confers the right to speak on the holder.

Religious Education

As stated at the beginning of the chapter, the Education Reform Act 1988 set out the need for education to 'promote the spiritual, moral, cultural, mental and physical development of pupils'. While Personal and Social Development offers a means of addressing the second of these areas, Religious Education (RE) provides teachers of pupils over the age of 5 with a means of addressing the first and the second.

The moral dimension of RE offers considerable potential for overlap between this subject and the more secular area of personal and social development. Both are concerned with helping children to develop notions of correct and incorrect forms of behaviour. RE can provide opportunities to help children develop their understanding of what it means to be fair, considerate, courageous and truthful, through introducing children to some of the stories associated with a range of religious faiths. However, RE also incorporates a spiritual dimension (Edwards and Knight, 1997). This aspect of RE involves both concepts (such as life after death, creation and miracles) and knowledge and understanding of the many different religions in Britain today including Christianity, Islam, Hinduism, Judaism, Buddhism and Sikhism.

Promoting knowledge and understanding of different religions with young children

- Visit the Commission for Racial Equality's website (www.cre.gov.uk), which contains pages offering information on ethnic and religious groups in Britain plus their history.
- Celebrate a range of religious festivals such as Eid, Diwali and Christmas.
- Tell stories as ways to celebrate with, and introduce young children to, the diversity and range of religious ideas and beliefs.

- Present religious ideas with respect if they are not to become indistinguishable from nursery rhymes and fairy stories. Unlike 'Goldilocks and the Three Bears', religious events and stories are underpinned by important articles of faith and belief.
- Invite visitors of different faiths to explain to children what it means to live life, for example, as a Muslim or a Christian.
- Discuss any special books associated with different religious faiths, for example the Bible, Qur'an or Torah.
- Discuss conventions and procedures associated with different religious faiths such as special preparations needed before entering a church, mosque or synagogue.
- Visit places of worship to look at the structure, architecture, designs, symbols, and objects (both functional and symbolic).
- Liaise with local representatives of different faiths, have clear learning objectives for planned visits and discuss them with these representatives.

Language and Literacy

AUDIT

By the end of this section you should

- have a broad understanding of the nature of literacy/English in the 3–8 curriculum and how to teach it (A2e-g, B5bii, B5c).

This area of learning forms a huge part of the 3–8 curriculum. Not only do language and literacy have a distinct identity of their own, they are involved in some way in almost every other activity that takes place in nursery or school. There can be few aspects of the 3–8 curriculum more important than literacy for children's future educational achievements and opportunities in life. However, unlike the other annexes in the Standards for initial teacher training, Annex C on English does not contain any specific statements relating to 3–8 teachers. Yet, while many statements are clearly inappropriate for the 3–8 age range, there are other elements in Annex C with great relevance for teachers and trainees working with this age group. This section will deal with the areas of speaking and listening, reading and writing. It will identify some of the key issues that 3–8 teachers need to consider and direct readers to further sources of information that they ought to familiarize themselves with in order to meet fully the Standards for initial teacher training.

Speaking and listening

Many children entering nursery or reception classes are relatively skilled in speaking and listening, having had experience of listening to stories, learning rhymes or singing along with songs on the radio or television at home. At the same time, some of their peers are lacking in confidence and can be reluctant to communicate. They may have difficulty in listening attentively for even the shortest of periods, and may also have only a very limited vocabulary. Other children may be fluent speakers and listeners, but not in English. This wide range of ability results in a great deal of time spent in providing opportunities designed to promote speaking and listening (DfEE, 1990). As children move through the 3–8 age range they should

- gain in confidence in their use of language;
- be able to demonstrate listening behaviour;
- be able to use language to describe, question, recall and recount their experiences;
- increase their ability to comprehend and communicate; and
- become more skilful in articulating and expressing their feelings and ideas verbally.

The ethos and environment in 3–8 settings play a crucial part in fostering children's speaking and listening skills. It is vital that young children have the confidence to talk.

Dealing with a reluctant speaker

When Matthew joined the reception class he was very reluctant to contribute verbally in front of his peers and others, so much so, that he would approach the teacher and whisper any questions or requests in her ear. His teacher realized that she would need to make Matthew feel secure and raise his confidence through patience, praise and quiet encouragement. The process took a great deal of time but by the end of the year Matthew felt able to join in group discussions and answer questions with support.

Such confidence can be developed through adult–child and child–child interactions where children are encouraged to talk about those things they are most familiar with, such as

- their experiences at home;
- what they are doing in the nursery/classroom;
- looking and talking about the things around them;
- thinking aloud about why things are the way they are; and
- being encouraged to approach teachers, other adults and peers to ask questions and make requests.

Conversations with peers and adults can improve children's abilities to describe, to remember, and to develop and clarify their thoughts and ideas. Discussions such as these also foster the ability to listen to the ideas and observations of their peers and others, as well as providing opportunities to introduce new vocabulary. In the case of pupils whose first language is not English, making effective use of bilingual teachers and support workers is also an effective strategy for raising confidence.

Increasing pupil confidence in speaking and listening

- Encourage children to
    ask and answer questions;
    seek information and clarification;
    retell and share personal experiences;
    participate in group discussions; and
    work cooperatively and collaboratively with their peers, in pairs and groups, during
    activities such as circle time or through socio-dramatic play in the home corner.
- Offer less threatening opportunities for children to express themselves verbally such as
  daily chats and discussions with small groups and individuals. This can be particularly
  rewarding for children who find talking in large groups (i.e. whole class situations)
  difficult and are thus reluctant to contribute.
- Use puppets, telephones and masks to help some children overcome their anxieties
  about speaking in public.

Questioning by teachers is also valuable in promoting good dialogue and interaction with and amongst pupils, and children need to be allowed the opportunity to ask questions as well as answer them.

Questioning

- Use more open-ended questions to provide opportunities for children to talk at length
  on a topic. Such questions offer more children the chance to respond and can be a
  good way of challenging more able pupils.
- Use closed questions (where there is one correct answer and what is being sought is
  more clearly defined) to offer greater security for some children.
- Having asked a question, do not be tempted to cut off the reply through impatience.
  Those teaching the 3–8 age range have to be prepared to wait and avoid jumping in
  too quickly to answer their own questions. Prompting can be helpful when children are
  making an effort to express themselves verbally, but if done too often or too quickly it
  can be frustrating for a child who knows the word(s) they need; they just want a second
  or two to remember and arrange them. At the same time, be sensitive to children who
  are genuinely struggling and be ready to support them when necessary.

Adults are constantly putting young children into situations where they need to pay attention. Listening carefully (individually, and in group and class situations) is an essential learning skill, yet it can prove a challenge for some young children.

Encouraging listening behaviour in children

- Establish speaking and listening conventions such as *hands up* and reward appropriate
  behaviour with praise and recognition.
- Issue simple instructions to encourage children to demonstrate attentiveness and
  respond appropriately to the speaker, for example when getting changed for dance and
  movement, washing hands before lunch, or putting on aprons before painting. These

routines and procedures, whilst being effective as class management strategies, are also an important part of the learning process.

- Provide musical activities to reinforce listening behaviour: for example, listening to and describing different types of sounds made by pluckers and shakers.
- Offer children practice in listening at story times or when singing rhymes and songs as a group or class, many of which involve accompanying actions requiring listening skills if they are to be performed at the correct time and in the right way.
- Create structured play areas in the classroom where children can use their verbal communication skills through participation in imaginary play, acting out a variety of roles and make-believe situations, and organizing and planning scenes using various props.

Speaking and listening in multi-cultural/bilingual contexts

Many schools and nurseries have pupils for whom English is not a first language. These children are far from being part of a homogeneous group. Such pupils may be bilingual or even multi-lingual; alternatively they may be at the very earliest stages of English acquisition. They may have very diverse backgrounds linguistically, socially and culturally and may well have different levels of language competency both in their mother tongue and in English. Failure to appreciate this diversity could result in teachers concluding, wrongly, that children have behavioural problems of some kind, or are less motivated or less intelligent than their English-speaking peers. It is important to realise that recognizing and supporting the breadth of their language skills and understanding will make a positive contribution to their learning of English and their success in education generally. At the same time, it is essential for all children to make progress in mastering English in the interests of their future achievements in school and, later on, their opportunities as adults.

Supporting speaking and listening in multi-cultural/bilingual contexts

- Where possible make use of bilingual support staff in the nursery/classroom. Children can be supported in taking in and understanding the spoken word, and can be encouraged to express themselves clearly and appropriately. Such support can help children overcome feelings of isolation and frustration where much of what goes on in the nursery/classroom may pass them by.
- Provide a learning environment in which children feel able to utilize the full range of their linguistic repertoire and feel confident that their first language has a legitimacy in the classroom (Barratt-Pugh, 1994).
- Provide resources including books, posters and ICT software that are free from cultural bias and negative, stereotypical images.
- Use dual-language books and tapes to give parity of esteem to other languages.
- Provide play equipment such as clothing, construction kits and artefacts that reflect a wide range of cultural experiences.
- Ensure that displays, labelling and written communication with children and their families reflect the diversity and variety of young children's home languages.

Reading and writing

Reading and writing are interdependent areas of learning. As with speaking and listening the range of ability in terms of reading and writing in 3–8 settings can be very wide. Some children upon entering nursery are able to recognize their own names in print and to engage in mark-making on paper which closely resembles writing. A few may even be able to read and write simple words such as their own names. By the time children move on to Key Stage 1 they should have improved their understanding of the functions of print, be experimenting with it, be using books and a variety of texts for pleasure and information, and be actively seeking and engaging in literary experiences.

Below is a broad brush model of the stages that young children go through in becoming readers and writers. Trainee and newly qualified teachers will need to refer to the further sources of information in order to understand completely and appreciate in full this area of children's learning.

Stages in becoming readers and writers

1. Emergent readers/writers, while taking part in shared activities with the teacher, are beginning to realize that writing and drawing are different means of communication, and that speech can be recorded in print and that print can be turned back into speech. They are beginning to learn some of the letter shapes, to write their names and to recognize familiar logos and signs in their local environment. They can move on to identify a handful of the more common words encountered in books such as 'is', 'and', 'the', and are also learning to recognize these words in isolation. Establishing attractive and stimulating reading and mark-making areas are important strategies in fostering a positive approach to reading and writing at this stage of children's development.

2. Beginning readers/writers are able to write their own name plus a small number of common words. They are also learning to recognize an increasing number of these common words such as 'in', 'my', 'her'. They are starting to join in much more with reading and discussion of stories, are beginning to blend sounds into words, can play I-spy games, and can match a range of words and letters by sight.

3. Developing readers/writers are beginning to read and write independently. They are able to use the context of a text and initial letters in their efforts to establish meaning, can read and write individual letters as well as an increasing range of words e.g. 'dog', 'cat', 'red'. As the children progress they become increasingly adept at using the context of a text to predict meaning and to work out more complicated phonic blends. They can read and write words with consonant blends (st, fr, sk, and, sl), consonant (ch, sh, th) and vowel (ea, oi) digraphs and are aware of the silent 'e' (like, come). They have a more extensive and increasing sight vocabulary. Although children's reading and writing development are interrelated it is worth remembering that developing readers and writers may be able to read more complex words than they can spell.

4. Fluent readers/writers have successfully achieved the basic competences. They can select books on the basis of interest and need. They can read and write words involving silent letters, longer word endings and polysyllabic words, and they can self-correct in reading.

Promoting reading and writing in 3–8 settings

- Provide opportunities for children to select books for individual needs and interests, and to request favourite stories in order to help them to become increasingly enthusiastic about using books for pleasure and information.
- When trying to help children to become increasingly knowledgeable about the functions of print, provide opportunities for them to see that written language has meaning.
- Encourage children to seek information about the meaning of print, and to attempt their own writing and to share texts.
- Establish an environment in the nursery/classroom where written text is used in meaningful ways such as recognizing familiar signs, labels and names.
- Encourage children to read and reread known simple texts.
- Take care not to rush the youngest children prematurely into formal approaches to reading and writing. In many nurseries, for example, reading and mark-making areas are set up to encourage children to engage in and enjoy the earliest stages of reading and writing in more informal settings.
- Set up a reading area in the nursery/classroom.
  - Offer a wide range of texts to appeal to the widest possible audience and extend pupils' experience (e.g. fiction, picture books, dual language texts, poems and rhymes, reference and non-fiction books, 'books' that the children have written themselves).
  - Display the books attractively to encourage children to select them, (e.g. using book boxes to present front covers rather than spines).
  - Provide comfortable seating and carpeting to encourage children to spend time in the area.
  - Include audio materials and ICT equipment such as story tapes and talking books.
- Set up a writing/mark-making area in the nursery/classroom.
  - Give the children a wide range of good quality mark making resources to encourage their involvement and to demonstrate the status such activities have in the teacher's mind (offer a wide variety of pencils, pens and crayons, and good quality paper).
  - Provide a range of real-life writing materials and artefacts (e.g. printed stationery, envelopes, labels, greetings cards, forms, tags, stamps, post-box) to help pupils see that writing has a purpose. Include scissors, tape, paper-clips, stapler, notice board and marker pens.
  - Give children access to a computer or other word processing equipment, (e.g. the concept keyboard).

Mathematics

AUDIT

By the end of this section you should

- have a broad understanding of the nature of mathematics in the 3–8 curriculum and how to teach it (A2e-g, B5d, Annex D B5a);

- know about the importance of pupils in nursery and reception classes acquiring the basic mathematical concepts necessary for later progression in mathematics, including

  recognizing and using numbers (Annex D A1a);

  comparing and recognizing relationships (Annex D A1b);

  ordering and sequencing (Annex D A1c);

  sorting and classifying (Annex D A1d);

  establishing invariant properties (Annex D A1e);

  using mathematical language (Annex D A1f);

  using mathematical knowledge to carry out simple number operations and solve practical problems (Annex D A1g).

Like language and literacy, mathematics is a powerful means of communication with importance and application across the curriculum. The inclusion of mathematics in the 3–8 curriculum provides opportunities to improve and increase children's powers of logical thinking, their ability to calculate, represent, explain and predict, as well as developing their spatial awareness. Many day-to-day nursery and school experiences of young children, including play, provide opportunities for learning mathematical ideas.

Number

From birth children are surrounded by ideas in number form. Number concepts which develop in the early years are the result of both teaching and informal experiences. Children come to attach meaning to number names as a result of frequent use in different contexts, such as sorting activities with beads and cotton reels, matching activities with collections of natural objects, counting games, and songs and rhymes involving numbers. Much early number work concerns correspondence and conservation, while using number names encourages the beginnings of understanding cardinal and ordinal numbers.

Early number exercises

- Make number collections
- Thread coloured beads following a sequence card
- Number rhymes and songs
- Count on/back

- Number 'jumps'
- One more than/less than
- Number patterns
- Simple number bonds, 1–5 leading to 5–10
- Number trails inside/outside the nursery/classroom
- Collecting groups of objects (e.g. 4 bricks, 3 leaves, 5 cars)
- Counting to 5, counting to 10.

Teachers of younger pupils need to appreciate the importance of children understanding number, and avoid confusing this with formal number operations and recording. Hughes (1986) presents a revealing insight into children's use of written arithmetic and suggests that there may be a disturbing discrepancy between children's use of symbols in the classroom and their ability to apply them elsewhere. Time is needed for children to relate their concrete understanding of number to the abstract written symbols.

Helping children with number

- Assist children to develop their skills in mental number work and provide opportunities to develop their understanding and skills still further through practical work.
- Offer pupils activities leading to counting; without the ability to count progress in children's general mathematical development will be severely limited.
- Take advantage of the myriad of counting opportunities that present themselves during the course of any day in a nursery or classroom.
    'How many?'
    'Who is second/third?'
    'Who has the most/least?'
    'Is it the same as/more than/less than?'
- View computational skills as tools. Children need not only the ability to perform a particular numerical operation, but also knowledge of when it should be employed. Many teachers will be familiar with questions such as 'Is it an add, Miss?' as some children struggle to make sense of written symbols, particularly operator signs such as + and –.
- Offer children opportunities to record in a variety of ways, including ways that relate to their mental work (DfEE, 1995). Encourage children to try out their own mental strategies. Many strategies can lead to the 'right answer'.
- Emphasize the importance of thinking mathematically (understanding, interpreting and communicating solutions) as well as standard calculation procedures.

Providing Practical Experience of Mathematics

Although mathematical operations such as addition and subtraction are crucially important, real and relevant contexts within which children have to exercise their mathematical skills are equally valuable.

Practical mathematics tasks

- Find and match bricks in the construction kits that are the same
- Compare (two objects to begin with)
- Work with foodstuffs, follow simple recipes
- Look for 'big' leaves and 'little' leaves in the environment
- Pass the parcel 'quickly' and 'slowly'
- Run on the spot in PE for a 'long' time and a 'short' time
- 'Which is the biggest/smallest?'
- 'Which container holds the most?'
- Arrange and rearrange play figures
- Sort and classify objects according to type, e.g. sort toy animals or cars as part of small-scale structured play activities
- Sort and classify objects according to shape, e.g. two-dimensional card cutouts, three-dimensional construction bricks
- Sort and classify objects according to colour, e.g. beads, bobbins
- Sort and classify objects according to size, e.g. containers in sand and water play
- Sort/group each other, e.g. 'Who's got laces on their shoes?' 'Who's got brown hair?'

Practical mathematical experiences can include work on shape and space, measurement, number work and logic. Many everyday activities in 3–8 classes provide opportunities to think logically and solve practical problems using mathematics. Using everyday routines and situations provides real contexts for the use of mathematics, for example, sharing out biscuits at milk time. The skills of prediction, classification, and sequencing can be encouraged through questions such as 'What will happen?' and 'Why do you think?' during structured play activities. Furthermore, everyday sorting and classifying activities can be useful in developing early logic. Children's logical thinking begins to develop as they start to distinguish differences and similarities in things, making comparisons and arranging them systematically.

Providing a practical dimension to mathematics

Offer children activities which require them to
- make direct comparisons (e.g. small and large, long and short);
- sequence more than two objects;
- measure (e.g. mix and combine materials such as foodstuffs or paint);
- utilize their estimation skills when measuring and/or comparing;
- move and handle a range of equipment and objects as a way of improving their spatial awareness of and developing an appreciation of patterns and relationships in shape and number;
- engage in structured play activities, including outdoor play and work with construction kits, to develop their awareness of shape and space.

Numeracy and the Whole Curriculum

Linking mathematics with other curriculum areas also provides opportunities for skills to be used in practical and meaningful situations, for example, measuring and marking out in design and technology, or using simple charts to record scientific observations. Nursery and reception teachers, in particular, are adept at drawing mathematical experiences out of activities that are ostensibly creative, scientific or physical in nature.

Establishing links with language and literacy is of prime importance. A great many stories, poems and songs that are used with young children provide ways of exposing them to mathematical ideas, knowledge and understanding, for example 'There Were Ten In The Bed'. The relationship between language and mathematics is particularly important. When children fail to understand what is being asked of them they will not be able to complete the activity they have been given. Adult–pupil talk provides numerous opportunities to encourage young children to think mathematically about

- number – 'Have we got enough?';
- measurement – 'Which is longer?';
- logic – 'Why did that happen?';
- spatial awareness – 'Which brick will fit in there?';
- mathematical language – 'Who's is the tallest/heaviest?', 'Who's got the most/least?'

Opportunities for mathematical learning are also present in many other activities that take place across the 3–8 curriculum.

Good exercises in mathematical learning

- Match objects in collections (leaves, seeds)
- Sort clothes in the home corner (hats, coats, gloves)
- Match objects in structured play activities (plates, cups)
- Create different structures/shapes with the same number of Lego bricks
- Create activities including songs and rhymes which involve counting by rote to give plenty of opportunity for practice ('Currant Buns in The Baker's Shop')
- Create large-scale play activities (setting up the Three Bears' house in the home corner).

Promoting mathematical skills, knowledge and understanding in 3–8 settings

- Provide opportunities for the acquisition and reinforcement of mathematical knowledge through practical work:
  - observe and talk about numerals around the classroom (the clock, plastic coins, number lines, including telephone numbers in a structured play area, talking about page numbers in books).
  - accompany the children on maths trails in the local environment (bus numbers, numbers on houses and cars).

- Provide opportunities for young children to engage in discussions on mathematical topics as a means of improving their understanding.
- Offer counting and number games, which you have planned and prepared, to provide opportunities for the children to engage in skills practice and for you to explain mathematical ideas.
- Use the medium of structured play with a wide range of equipment such as sand, water, construction kits and toys to provide investigative and problem-solving experiences .
- Remember the importance of opportunities for consolidation and reinforcement, rather than rushing into, and insisting upon, formal recording too quickly, especially with younger children.
- Set up a numeracy area in the nursery/classroom. The resources could include
  - counting materials (beads, buttons, number lines);
  - blocks, shapes, sorting games and jigsaws;
  - measuring equipment (rulers, metre sticks, scales and balances, clocks and timers);
  - maths books and stories with a mathematical theme;
  - writing/drawing materials.

Knowledge and Understanding of the World

AUDIT

By the end of this section you should

- be familiar with Knowledge and Understanding of the World in the Desirable Outcomes, and science, design and technology, geography and history in the National Curriculum (A2e-g);

- have acquired an understanding of how to teach these subjects to 3–8 pupils (A2e-g, B5biii);

- recognize the importance of providing pupils in nursery and reception classes with opportunities to

  - recognize the features of living things, objects, materials and events in the natural and made world, including looking closely at similarities, differences, patterns and change (Annex E, A2a);

  - gain information about why things happen and how things work (Annex E, A2b);

  - talk and think critically and creatively about their observations and begin to record them with adult support (Annex E, A2c);

  - select and use materials and equipment, and take turns and cooperate when using equipment (Annex E, A2d);

  - use technology to support their learning in science (Annex E, A2e).

Young children are fascinated by the natural phenomena and manufactured objects that they see around them on a daily basis. By introducing practical activities which enable children to use their senses, 3–8 teachers can help to lay some of the foundations for understanding in geography, history, technology, and science.

Science

First-hand experiences and observations of the world around them provide children with opportunities to foster positive attitudes towards investigation and experimentation, such as curiosity and perseverance. With young children this can relate to a range of topics including materials and their properties, similarities and differences, patterns and changes, living things and forces. At the same time early first-hand experiences also present opportunities to acquire a range of skills useful in science once children encounter the National Curriculum, including

- critical thinking (asking questions about why and how things happen, predicting);
- problem-solving and investigating;
- observational skills;
- measuring, sorting and classifying; and
- hypothesizing (talking about their observations, identifying cause and effect).

A taste of science

A class of Y1/2 children had been doing work on the theme of Ourselves. They had been investigating the five senses. The children had a small selection of plastic pots each of which held a similar looking white material – sugar, salt, icing sugar, self-raising flour and cornflour – to be identified by smell, touch and taste. They described what the substances smelled and felt like and one of the children said that the salt and sugar were 'all crunchy'. The teacher asked the children to look very closely at the different materials to see if they were really that similar. During the subsequent discussion the teacher introduced the words *powder* and *crystal*. The children then compared the taste. Some were easily identified (salt and sugar), others (flour and cornflour) were unknown to the children. One child then asked what would happen if they mixed in some water. The teacher seized the opportunity to extend the children's learning further in the area of materials and their properties. They were asked to predict what would happen and then she added some water to the pots and stirred the mixtures. The children noticed that some of the substances seemed to disappear. The teacher asked the children to taste the liquids and the children observed that they could still taste the sugar and salt even though they had apparently disappeared. The teacher then introduced the word *dissolve*.

When engaged in early science activities, children should be encouraged to become increasingly responsible for handling equipment and resources safely and sensibly. This could include selecting and collecting objects to see if they will float or sink, putting magnets back where they came from with their keepers attached, and keeping their work area reasonably tidy. When children are making these choices and exercising their decision-making abilities, they need to do so in an environment that is inherently safe.

Using equipment safely

- Do not allow children access to hot materials or sharp tools without close adult supervision.
- Remind children about the hazards of tasting or smelling strange materials and liquids.
- Use plastic containers not glass ones.
- Use water-based glues not solvents.
- Warn children of the dangers of mains electricity.

Early science activities also provide learning opportunities across the 3–8 curriculum. Personal and social development can be fostered by enabling and encouraging young children to work harmoniously and sensibly with their peers. Praise and recognition can make children aware that listening to others, offering ideas and observations, carefully following instructions, and considerately sharing tasks are all valued behaviours. At the same time, encouraging and assisting young children in recording science activities provides opportunities to foster the development of their communication skills, as well as providing teachers with concrete evidence with which to support the assessment, recording and reporting of children's learning. Having to *write up* experiments and investigations upon completion can be problematic with very young children, not to say inappropriate on occasions. A written account is not always the most suitable method for recording science work. Some investigative work with young children may not warrant a permanent record and in such cases children can be encouraged to talk about their work and their observations. Many young children will be emergent writers. To produce written work at the end of science tasks could well reduce their interest in and enthusiasm for the subject. Some investigations could be recorded in an ongoing rather than a summative form, such as keeping a daily record of the weather or the growth of cress seeds. Where a written account is appropriate, teachers can act as scribes for those children who need this level of support. Other options for recording early science work in ways that best suit the task include: pre-prepared charts and simple tables, diagrams, pictures, photographs, tape recordings and cooperative or group reports.

More 3–8 science activities

- **Sound and music**. Make shakers using rice and peas, 'guitars' using boxes and elastic bands.
- **Magnets**. Which materials are attracted to magnets? Can the children move objects with a magnet at a distance, for example through the tabletop, through a sheet of paper?
- **Investigating soaps and detergents**. Make bubbles and get things clean.
- **Light and colour**. Make shadows using torches. Do a science walk around the school/nursery looking at the use of colour in the local environment (for example shop fronts, road signs and traffic lights).

- **Materials and their properties/similarities and differences**. Introduce a reception class to different sorts of paper (writing paper, newsprint, cards, wall papers and gift wrap), and encourage them to describe the different properties such as texture, colour and pattern. Use these different types of paper in a range of contexts.
- **Living things**. Visit a local park and collect objects such as autumn fruits and leaves. Talking about the seasons to provide opportunities to raise the children's awareness of range and diversity. Year 1 children can use a commercially produced database to find out about animals as part of a project on pets.
- **Patterns and changes**. Work with foodstuffs, mix the materials and heat them.
- **Forces**. Rolling toy cars down ramps at various angles with Year 2 pupils. Water play with nursery/reception pupils, testing objects to see which ones float and which ones sink, making floaters sink and sinkers float.

Design and Technology

There are many links between science and design and technology but they are not one and the same thing (Davies, 1997). Young children need opportunities to develop their technology skills by designing and making, as well as developing their scientific understanding by observing and investigating the world around them. Much design in the early stages of a child's education is changeable, based on trial and error; it often runs concurrently with making and the products themselves can be ephemeral in nature, such as sand structures.

Evolution of a child's idea

During a nursery placement a student teacher was asked to work with children engaged in a construction activity using junk materials and paint. She asked one child about his model and he replied that it was a fire engine. Later in the session the student teacher praised the child's construction (a series of cardboard boxes, glued together and painted bright red). 'That's a fantastic fire engine you've made.' 'It's not a fire engine,' the child replied indignantly, 'it's a lighthouse.'

A good range of low-cost and no-cost materials (i.e. card boxes, yogurt pots, lolly sticks) are invaluable in giving children opportunities to select and make decisions. At the same time, augmenting such materials with more sophisticated commercially-produced resources such as construction kits gives children a chance to model with an accuracy that would otherwise be far beyond them. Work with food can be particularly useful. It allows young children to design and make with materials that are accessible, exciting, easily worked and that offer a wide range of possible outcomes. Introducing food activities can also provide opportunities to introduce a multi-cultural dimension to the 3–8 curriculum but teachers should know the food rules of different cultures and faith communities.

Some ideas for food activities

Taste different breads and fillings and then make sandwiches.
Taste a variety of breads then bake bread. Add different ingredients and flavourings to
   the dough.
Make a green salad or fruit salad.
Make butter.
Make fruit yogurt by adding fruit to a plain yogurt base.
Cook eggs in different ways.
Make vegetable soup.
Make a pizza.
Make drinks (e.g. tea, coffee, cocoa, fruit juice, milkshakes).
Make festive foods and food presents.
Add beans, salad ingredients and dressings to rice, bulghar wheat or cous-cous.
Make baked potatoes with different fillings.
Make a teddy bears' picnic meal.
Make different coloured peppermint creams.

Children's health and safety is an important factor in design and technology
activities where potentially harmful tools and equipment may be involved.

Health and safety in design and technology

• Trainee and newly qualified teachers should consult the nursery/school health and
  safety guidelines when planning design and technology activities.
• Children should be shown how to handle tools properly.
• Certain tools and equipment should only be used under adult supervision. Young
  children can use knives but only under close supervision. All tools must be stored out of
  reach when not needed.
• Some tools should only be used by the teacher or another responsible adult.

Establishing clear boundaries

The woodwork bench in the nursery had a range of soft timber offcuts, two pots
of nails, two hammers, two saws and two vices. Teaching and non-teaching staff
taught the children how to hold and use the saws properly and safely, how to put
timber in a vice and how to use a hammer to drive a nail into wood. When an
adult was present in the area children could opt to experiment with the tools and
materials. When there was no adult there a thick blanket was placed over the
whole bench and children knew that the activity was off-limits.

Avoiding unnecessary risks

A reception teacher was setting up a structured play area in her classroom. The
theme was 'The launderette' and the children were constructing some of the
artefacts to go into the area, gaining experience of handling tools and materials in
the process. One group was making a washing machine from a large cardboard

box. They drew round a plastic plate to show where the door needed to go but the card was too thick for scissors, so the teacher did the cutting for them using a craft knife which was always kept securely locked away. Children were not allowed to use it, even under supervision.

- When working with food, surfaces must be clean, hands must be washed and allergies (such as nut allergies) need to be borne in mind.
- When using heat sources children should not move hot liquids. Microwave ovens provide opportunities to make some dishes more safely, easily and quickly.

As with early science work, work in design and technology can contribute to children's learning in other areas:

- Children can begin to hone their abilities in reasoning and thinking logically as well as their interpersonal skills such as cooperation, sharing and negotiation.
- Children can consider the aesthetic side of design by being encouraged to make things which are artistically appealing as well as purely functional thus making connections between their creative development and their knowledge and understanding of the world.
- Designing and making activities can give children the chance to apply knowledge and skills gained in English and mathematics, for example measuring before cutting, 'buying' materials with budgets, and discussing their plans.
- Local walks and visits provide opportunities for young children to observe the wider made environment, including such things as street furniture, machines and buildings. Imaginative and investigative play can be also be used to develop children's interest in the technological products they see around them.
- Technology can be used to support children's learning in science. For example
  – collect moving toys (e.g. battery powered and mechanically powered using clockwork motors, or stored energy in springs) and investigate what makes them work;
  – use the computer to record daily weather conditions.

Setting up a design and technology area in the nursery/classroom

Textile equipment
- large needles (some pre-threaded)
- variety of threads, silks and wool
- hessian and binka fabrics, patterned offcuts
- scissors (for textile use only, paper blunts scissors quickly)
- miscellaneous materials (ribbon, elastic, buttons, feathers, beads and sequins)
- baskets for storage

Work with more resistant materials
- tools (scissors, hole punchers, staplers, pliers, vices, hammers, bench hooks, glass paper/sanders, saws, drills and glue guns for use under supervision only)
- joining materials (good quality PVA adhesive, Sellotape, masking tape, string, paper fasteners, elastic bands, nails)
- more resistant materials (dowelling, soft timber, balsa, wooden wheels)
- less resistant and found materials (cardboard boxes, plastic bottles and containers, card wheel, lollysticks, cotton bobbins)

Construction equipment

- large-scale materials (Bau Spiel, Tac-Tic, large wooden blocks)
- small-scale materials (Lego, Duplo-Toolo)
- instruction sheets (remove for free play; include for more directed tasks)
- extension materials for small-scale play activities (plastic figures, floor maps)
- extension materials for large-scale play activities (role-play materials)

Geography and History

Geography and history can be fascinating for young children. Although at first glance teachers may find it hard to relate their adult understanding of these subjects to their practice in nursery and infant classrooms, a great deal of potential exists in the 3–8 curriculum for using geography and history to make the curriculum relevant to young children while simultaneously laying the foundations for later learning (Edwards and Knight, 1994).

Geography is much more than simply memorizing and locating different places. It is a way for young children to study the world around them. Geography involves knowledge and understanding about the interaction between the environment and people, as well as developing a set of enquiry-based skills.

Geographical concepts and skills

- pattern
- processes and systems
- similarities and differences
- asking questions
- collecting information
- interpreting and presenting information
- drawing conclusions

History involves more than mastering a prescribed set of names, dates and events in the correct sequence. History offers children a way of understanding the past. This involves the introduction of key concepts and skills as well as the assimilation of particular pieces of information or *facts* (Edwards and Knight, 1997).

Historical concepts and skills

- There was a past
- The past was different from the present
- There was an order or sequence to the past
- In many cases (though not all) objects and information from the past remain and can help us to make sense of what things used to be like
- Finding out about other periods, asking and answering questions
- Interpreting historical events
- Organizing and communicating historical information

Children who are still coming to terms with concepts such as *earlier than*, *later than*, *yesterday*, *today* and *tomorrow* are not incapable of understanding the concepts of time or alternative places, provided teachers introduce them to these ideas in ways that are appropriate and manageable for them (DES, 1992).

Making geography and history relevant to young children

- Begin with the children. (What did you do yesterday? Where are you going at the weekend?)
- Work back to consider the family. (Discuss different generations in their family, different places they have lived.)
- Move on to consider the local area. (What was the local area like in the past? How has it changed?)
- Broaden the curriculum to consider the more distant past and locations. (Periods beyond living memory, national and international locations.)

In geography, learning can occur when you

- talk about and examine the immediate environment, including where the children live;
- read stories such as 'The Shopping Basket';
- make three-dimensional maps in the sand tray;
- use roll-out road maps in structured play;
- look at photographs, including aerial photographs of local places;
- go on local walks to introduce children to appropriate language such as *semi-detached*, *valley* and *church*;
- look at plan views of the classroom/school;
- make memory maps of how the children came to school;
- use secondary sources to find out about more distant places.

In history, learning can occur when you

- talk about past and present events in the children's own lives;
- *interview* older relatives about how things used to be;
- make family timelines and albums;
- collect and display artefacts from previous times (coins, stamps, posters, tickets);
- discuss and compare past and present artefacts (collecting toys that parents and grandparents may have kept from their own childhood and comparing them with toys today);
- look at and discussing old photographs and postcards of the local area;
- visit local historical sites to consider how and why people and places have altered over time;
- use secondary sources to find out about the more distant past.

KNOWLEDGE AND UNDERSTANDING

Physical development and physical education (PE)

By the end of this section you should

- have begun to understand how pupils' learning is affected by their physical development (A2c);
- have an overview of PE in the National Curriculum and how to teach it (A2e,f,g, B5biv).

Between the ages of 3 and 8 children make considerable progress in their coordination, manipulation and muscular control. (Sharman, *et al.*, 1998) Physical development is a major part of the early years curriculum as children's physical development is intimately connected to their intellectual and academic progress. Growing confidence in their physical abilities can promote a growing confidence and self-esteem across the curriculum. Children who have not been able to practise using their bodies with increasing levels of skill can experience difficulties in other areas of learning as they progress through nursery and school.

By the time children enter nursery/reception classes most already have an understanding and awareness of their bodies and their physical competence. The physical education, dance and movement, and play activities that they enjoy in nursery or school constitute much more than ways of letting young and active children burn off excess energy.

Aims of physical development and physical education:

- to encourage children to develop positive attitudes and confidence about themselves and their physical abilities;
- to ensure that children are safe and secure both physically and emotionally;
- to provide an environment which allows children to develop a degree of autonomy and independence; and
- to promote progress in physical development across a broad range, including gross and fine motor control, hand–eye coordination, body awareness, sensory awareness, spatial awareness, safety awareness, hygiene and healthy living.

Physical Development

Health and fitness form a central part of both physical development and the PE curriculum. When promoting good health practices teachers need to help pupils improve their understanding of how their bodies function and how to keep them healthy. Safety is essential. Teachers of young children have a legal obligation to keep pupils safe (see Chapter 4), an obligation that is much easier to fulfil if the children themselves are conscious of safety issues.

Promoting positive attitudes towards safety, health and fitness

- Require children to demonstrate appropriate hygiene practices such as washing their hands before going to lunch.
- Talk to children about different foods and the food/health connection.
- Talk to children about the positive effects of exercise.
- Teach children about the need to warm up and cool down, and help them learn about appropriate posture and use of their bodies.
- Give children opportunities to discuss safety and what it means, both for themselves and their peers. Such discussions could include revisiting and restating rules and conventions that help to create a safe environment.
- Encourage children to exercise their judgement and be assertive enough to be able to say no to others when their safety is at risk, as well as identifying and reporting unsafe resources and situations to their teachers.
- Insist on appropriate clothing. Wearing the right gear is one way to avoid accidents in PE. Teachers can reinforce this idea by changing into PE gear themselves, even if it only involves putting on a pair of trainers.
- Teach children to use, manipulate and move equipment safely (e.g. carry mats in fours).

Play can provide excellent opportunities to promote physical development. Sand and water play provide opportunities to extend and improve fine motor control as well as being a way to introduce pupils to scientific and mathematical ideas, to foster language and creative development, to encourage cooperative learning and personal and social development. Outdoor play provides opportunities to develop gross motor control and hand–eye coordination, and to engage in role-play. As with sand and water play, outdoor play not only promotes children's physical development but also enhances their development across the curriculum including their personal and social development, creative development and knowledge and understanding about the world.

Providing play opportunities for nursery and reception pupils

Water play
- Science and maths. Funnels, jugs, containers, water wheels, ice cubes, coloured water, washing-up liquid for bubbles.
- Language/ creativity. Plastic figures, boats.
- Health, hygiene and safety. Aprons, bucket, mop, cloths.

Sand play
- Science and maths. Spades and trowels, buckets, containers, spoons, rakes, damp and dry sand.
- Language/creativity. Plastic figures, toy vehicles.
- Health, hygiene and safety. Aprons, sweeping brush, dustpan.

Note: It is important to change the water or sand regularly and to ensure that equipment for clearing and cleaning up is readily to hand.

Outdoor play

Provide

- climbing and balancing apparatus;
- crates, wooden boxes, cubes;
- barrels, tunnels;
- planks, beams, slides;
- see-saws, rockers;
- hard and padded surfaces (mats under climbing apparatus);
- surfaces to promote games and play (hopscotch grids, targets on walls);
- tricycles, bicycles, scooters, wagons; and
- games apparatus (e.g. balls, bats, bean bags, quoits, hoops, rings).

Note: As with any activity involving potentially dangerous equipment, outdoor play needs proper adult supervision. This supervision includes not merely observing children during their play, but also creating a play environment that is not inherently dangerous.

Physical Education (PE)

As children move through the 3–8 age range and into the infant school they are introduced to more formal physical education lessons. Effective provision in PE offers children a range of indoor and outdoor activities that encourages them to respond confidently to physical challenges in a safe environment and enables them to become increasingly competent in the use of their bodies. PE can do much to increase young children's ability to engage in both cooperative and independent learning, as teachers encourage children to

- show consideration for their surroundings and peers;
- collaborate, share and negotiate with other children; and
- follow rules and play fairly.

PE involves children in planning, performing and evaluating physical activities in a range of contexts, including gymnastics, games and dance.

Games help children to develop their physical skills and understanding of simple tactics and rules.

In **dance and movement** children have the chance to develop actions, appreciate concepts such as fast and slow, learn to make effective use of personal and general space, and have opportunities for creativity and composition, for example, moving like an animal.

In **gymnastics** children learn and develop actions and movements that contribute to the development of their gross motor control and hand–eye coordination as they move from floor work to apparatus work.

Helping children to become increasingly proficient at planning and performing in PE

- Encourage and support children in taking calculated risks and offer praise for showing confidence and enjoyment in physical activity.

- Teach a range of physical skills and techniques.
- Be alert to children's capabilities and confidence and do not introduce tasks prematurely (for example, forward rolls) that will undermine confidence and enthusiasm.
- Promote positive attitudes towards health and fitness and an increased awareness of safety principles.
- Promote both cooperative and independent learning.
- Ask children to respond to tasks and try different ways of completing them.
- As pupils become more skilful, provide opportunities for them to start to link and combine actions and movements and plan more complex movements, sequences of movements and tactics in games, (rolling, bouncing, throwing and catching balls).

Helping children to evaluate their own, and others', achievements in PE as a means of improvement

Ask children to
- copy the actions and movements of their peers;
- describe their own and others' actions and movements;
- identify and comment on good work; and
- compare actions and movements, suggesting modifications and improvements.

Creative Development

AUDIT

By the end of this section you should

- know about Creative Development in the Desirable Outcomes, and art and music in the National Curriculum (A2e-g);
- have acquired an understanding of how to teach these subjects to 3–8 pupils (A2e-g, B5bv).

Young children respond well to sensory experience and the chance to experiment with tools, materials, sounds, shapes and colour. Creative work allows children to express their ideas and feelings, and to make sense of the world in a very practical way. It gives them experience of making choices and decisions, and promotes independence and perseverance. Through subjects such as art and music, and socio-dramatic role-play, pupils can develop their imagination, use materials creatively and appreciate beauty.

Music

Young children get great pleasure from playing and listening to music. Music is particularly useful as a way of helping children to acquire the vital learning skill of listening. It should be valued for the opportunities it offers to underpin learning in other areas of the curriculum such as mathematics (time, tempo, rhythm) as well as for its inherent worth. In 3–8 settings, a music table or trolley offers young children first-hand experience of a range of sounds and instruments.

Setting up a music table in the nursery/classroom

Provide:
- a range of instruments (tambourines, drums, cymbals, triangles, shakers, bells, chimebars, wind instruments)
- tape recorders and blank tapes for children to record and listen to their compositions
- taped songs, tunes and rhymes
- song books
- ICT music packages

Although there is certainly a technical element to music, teachers who do not possess technical skills can still be effective in helping children to enjoy and gain confidence in their creative musical abilities. Listening and responding to a range of musical expressions, including music from different cultures and periods, as well as discussing their feelings, helps to promote appreciation, knowledge and understanding, for example, of the difference between loud and quiet, fast and slow. Learning and singing rhymes and songs with accompanying actions, and using their bodies as instruments (clapping, tapping, clicking fingers) are also enjoyable and useful.

Singing songs and rhymes

- One, two, three, four, five, once I caught a fish alive
- Pat-a-cake, baker's man
- Incy Wincy Spider
- Row your boat
- I'm a little teapot
- I hear thunder
- Ring a ring o' roses
- If you're happy and you know it
- The wheels on the bus
- Heads and shoulders, knees and toes

Most children do not start formal instrumental music instruction before they are 8 or 9 years old. They should, however, be given opportunities to perform and compose music informally, and to experiment with and learn about the different sorts of sounds made by a range of instruments (percussion, string, wind). Access to computer software packages and programmable keyboard toys allow children to compose and listen to music. The instruments on offer to pupils in 3–8 settings can be real or home-made. Real instruments ought to originate from a wide variety of different cultures and locations to extend pupil's musical knowledge and understanding (*Let's Get it Right*, 1996).

Making simple instruments

- Shakers (boxes, plastic pop bottles, tins, thick paper bags, peas, beans, pasta shells, rice, buttons);
- drums (ice cream containers, plastic tubs and bowls, tins);
- chimes (metal objects on string such as knives and forks);
- pluckers (boxes/tins with elastic bands stretched across the top).

Art

Art offers excellent opportunities for the development of fine motor control and knowledge and understanding about the world as children are given opportunities to observe carefully, record natural and manufactured objects from a range of cultures and locations, and express their ideas and feelings visually. Through art children can explore, experiment and work with two- and three-dimensional materials in an imaginative manner, develop their abilities to handle tools and equipment safely and effectively, and learn useful techniques with which to express themselves. Art with young children should value and emphasize the process as well as the product, the ability to mix the paints and understand colour and texture for example, are important concomitants to the imaginative and expressive aspects of the subject.

Drawing and painting

By the time children reach the age of 3 many are beginning to want to draw rather than simply scribble. They often begin by trying to represent people they know, with end results often reminiscent of a 'Mr Man'.

As children get more practice and become more proficient, their drawings and paintings begin to include more detail; a person may now be shown to have a body or fingers. Children start to make decisions about what they will draw or paint prior to doing so, rather than deciding what a drawing or painting represents afterwards.

By the time the children are ready to move on from Key Stage 1 to Key Stage 2, most are able to incorporate a number of different objects in their pictures and include a rudimentary sense of perspective with houses, trees or clouds in the background.

It is important to remember that children's abilities in art vary, just as they do in other areas. Some pupils may be competent at drawing and thus capable of representing their observations/ideas at a level normally associated with older children. Others may have had fewer opportunities to experiment with drawing materials and, therefore, their pictures may be less well crafted than those of their peers.

The examples on pages 44 and 45 illustrate the sort of progression that can be seen in children's drawing skills. They are, however, intended to be indicative and should not be seen as definitive.

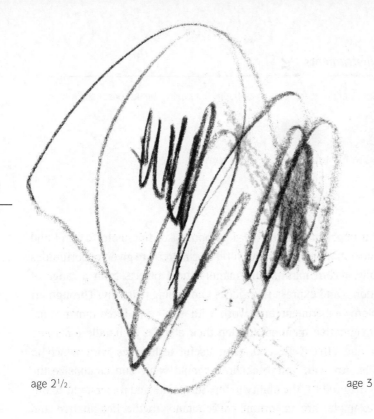

age 2½.

age 3

age 4

age 5

age 6

age 7

age 8

KNOWLEDGE AND UNDERSTANDING

Drawing materials
- pencils
- coloured pencils
- crayons
- felt tips and pens
- pastels
- chalks

Drawing activities
- wax crayon rubbings
- tracing round hands, feet
- making simple patterns
- observational drawings (KS1)

Painting and printing materials
- range of brushes
- sponges
- easels
- pots and palettes
- dry powder paints in primary colours

Painting and printing activities
- splatter painting (flicking paint onto paper using a small brush)
- blow painting (blowing runny paint around the paper using a drinking straw)
- finger painting
- wax paintings (drawing a picture with a white wax candle, painting over with a thin paint wash to reveal the outline)
- vegetable printing (potatoes can be cut to create simple shapes)
- block printing (styrofoam, clay, Plasticene, cotton bobbins)
- body printing (hands, feet, fingers)
- symmetrical printing (drip paint onto one half of the paper and fold over to create the final pattern, alternatively drape painting string onto one half of the paper and then fold)
- poster and powder paints in black, white and primary colours offer children the chance to experiment with a wide range of effects and to learn how to mix their own colours. Paints can be watered down or thickened using PVA adhesive, flour and water, or wallpaper paste (avoid fungicidal pastes)

Three-dimensional materials
- malleable materials for exploring form (clay, Plasticene, play dough. Play dough recipe: 2 parts plain flour, 1 part salt, 1 part cold water and 1 tablespoon vegetable oil)
- boards
- rolling pins, cutting tools, stamps
- collage materials

Three-dimensional activities
- collage
- mobiles
- mosaics
- greetings cards
- cutting doilies to make snowflakes;
- colour or scent the playdough for variety using food colourings and essences (make sure it does not tempt young children to consume it)

46

Early Information and Communications Technology (ICT)

AUDIT

By the end of this section you should

- have increased your knowledge and understanding of the content specified in the ICT National Curriculum for Information and Communications Technology (A2dvii);
- understand the importance of introducing pupils in nursery and reception classes to the use of ICT and recognize the contribution that ICT can make to this age group, including how to
  - encourage pupils to become familiar with ICT and to become positive users of it (Annex B, A9a);
  - ensure that all pupils have opportunities to use ICT, and that their experience takes account of any home use or other previous experience of ICT (Annex B, A9b);
  - identify and teach the skills necessary for handling input devices effectively (Annex B, A9c);
  - use ICT to support the development of language and literacy (Annex B, A9d);
  - use ICT to support the development of numeracy (Annex B, A9e);
  - use ICT to support pupils' creative development (Annex B, A9f);
  - encourage pupils working collaboratively with ICT to share responsibilities for making decisions and reaching conclusions (Annex B, A9g).

Although this does not form a separate area of experience within the Desirable Outcomes and Early Learning Goals, using ICT is given a more overt form within the National Curriculum, towards which young children are working, and it is also outlined in more detail within Circular 4/98 in Annex B. ICT involves more than just the computer. It incorporates any technology related to information and communication, including television, radio, audio and video cassettes, and faxes. Using ICT in 3–8 classes provides opportunities for interactive learning, the promotion of fine motor control, personal and social development and the development of reasoning skills. Using information and communications technology in a variety of ways and contexts helps children to become increasingly familiar with it, and increasingly confident and positive about their skills as users.

Increasing familiarity and confidence with ICT

- Place a computer in the role-play area and integrate it with structured play activities on different themes such as travel agent, bank, ticket office, theatre.
- Use off-site visits to draw attention to the use of ICT in the real world – the library, supermarket bar codes, concept keyboards in shops and fast food outlets.
- Send and receive faxes and e-mails with children.
- Introduce children to the world wide web as an information source.
- Use programmable toys such as the 'Roamer' or the 'Pixie'.

Young children are increasingly enthusiastic and proficient users of information technology. (DES, 1989) Many of them have access to ICT in the home and, not surprisingly, those that do are likely to make better progress in school and nursery. Some parents may not be fully aware of the place of ICT within their children's education and may not appreciate its relevance. Teachers may need to alert parents to the value of these experiences and discuss how to help children get the most out of ICT activities at home. Such discussions would also give teachers a chance to find out about the extent of their pupils' previous ICT experience and skills before planning to use ICT.

Increasing children's ICT skills

- Allow time for young children to master skills.
- Use commercially-produced software to introduce children to the keyboard in a structured and systematic fashion.
- Remember that keyboard skills will also develop as a consequence of using the computer in a variety of purposeful contexts, for example writing stories.
- Provide regular and frequent turns at operating the keyboard as this will be much more effective at increasing computer skills and confidence than infrequent but long turns.
- Use concept keyboards to replace the computer keyboard or to supplement it, with software that can be closed in nature or open ended, (allowing teachers to design their own overlays for their pupils).
- Introduce children to the mouse. Young children can become proficient quite quickly. Drawing packages are particularly useful in providing them with lots of practice.

The use of ICT in the nursery/classroom offers considerable potential for enriching and enhancing the whole curriculum. There is a clear correspondence between language and literacy and the strand of ICT associated with the communication of information. ICT also provides valuable tools for reinforcing the essential first-hand and practical mathematics experiences of young children. Children's creative development is underpinned and enriched through the inclusion of an ICT dimension. Computers provide yet another context within which young children can progress in terms of their personal and social development through being encouraged to work collaboratively with others.

Using ICT to support learning across the 3–8 curriculum

- Speaking and listening can be enhanced through the use of audio-taped stories and computerized books (talking books). Promoting collaborative (paired) work on the computer requires the children to contribute verbally to the completion of the task.
- Talking books can be used to support early reading as the children can hear the words on the screen. Software that involves matching objects to letters and finding the correct letters, such as 'My World' can also support reading. For older/more able pupils there is software to reinforce phonics.

- Writing can be supported through the use of ICT. Editing and redrafting benefit in particular. Software is also available that will demonstrate letter formation on the screen, and children can use the keyboard or a concept keyboard to produce emergent writing.
- Pupils' facility with number can be advanced through the use of simple operations programs.
- Work on shape, space and measurement can be supported through the use of shape naming programs, finding the positions of objects in packages like 'Albert's House', and work with the Roamer or other programmable devices.
- Using drawing and painting packages offers advantages for young children in terms of the quality of the finish and the opportunity to edit their art work in a way that does not require excessive use of materials or result in messy outcomes.
- Software also exists which enables young children to play and compose tunes, and raise their appreciation and awareness of a wide range of different types of music.

The teacher plays an important role in organizing and managing positive ICT experiences for all the children in the nursery/classroom. They must be ready to step in and intervene if necessary. It is easy to become complacent and blinded, by the obvious enthusiasm of some pupils, to the need to monitor and ensure quality in teaching and learning, not least in terms of equality of opportunity.

Organizing and managing ICT in the classroom

- Group children of similar ability, personalities and dispositions together to generate lively and rewarding discussion, where the pace tends to be agreed and children are less likely to be excluded.
- Use mixed ability pairs, particularly where there is a lot of reading to be done.
- Use children with previous ICT experience as an asset in groups, especially with younger children.
- Be alert to experienced children denying access to others. The warning signs include children making unilateral decisions; children monopolizing the keyboard; children operating the keyboard too quickly for their partner(s) to follow or understand; children bossing other children, generating disagreements and squabbles; and children being excluded or ignored by their peers.
- Try to observe the children soon after they have started working on the computer so that there is time to intervene at an early stage.
- Be prepared to alter groupings to ensure that pupils have positive collaborative experiences while working with ICT.
- Younger children work well in pairs in front of the computer. While threes are possible, more than three tends to lead to exclusion and lack of space to sit comfortably.
- Ensure that children have a clear role when working together on a computer. There are only really three roles possible:
  1. operating the keyboard
  2. reading the screen
  3. recording any information.
- Encourage children to have a turn in different roles to avoid individuals monopolizing control of the machine. The centre seat (the one in front of the keyboard) is where control is maintained. A change of role ought to be accompanied by a change of seat.

(Ellis, 1986)

Understanding the 3–8 Curriculum

Anning, A. (ed.) (1995) *A National Curriculum for the Early Years*. Buckingham: Open University Press.

Department for Education and Employment (1995) *Key Stages 1 and 2 of the National Curriculum*. London: HMSO.

Qualifications and Curriculum Authority (1998a) *Maintaining Breadth and Balance at Key Stages 1 and 2*. London: QCA Publications.

Qualifications and Curriculum Authority (1998b) 'Early Years', Conference Report. at www.qca.org.

Qualifications and Curriculum Authority (June 1999) 'Review of Desirable Learning Outcomes', Consultation Report. London: QCA Publications.

School Curriculum and Assessment Authority (1996) *Nursery Education Desirable Outcomes for Children's Learning on Entering Compulsory Education*. London: DfEE/SCAA.

Qualifications and Curriculum Authority (1999) *Investing in our Future: Early Learning Goals*. London: QCA

Rodger. R. (1999) *Planning an Appropriate Curriculum for the Under-5s*. London: David Fulton Publishers.

Understanding how young children learn

Athey, C. (1990) *Extending Thought in Young Children: A Parent–Teacher Partnership*. London: Chapman.

Bruce, T. (1997) E*arly Childhood Education* (2nd edn). London: Hodder and Stoughton.

Haylock, D. and Cockburn A. (1997) *Understanding Maths in Lower Primary Years*. London: Chapman.

Megginson, S. (1990) *Developing Role Play*. Rotherham Metropolitan Borough Council Department of Education.

Moyles, J. (1989) *Just Playing?*. Buckingham: Open University Press.

Nutbrown, C. (1994) *Threads of Thinking*. London: Chapman.

Osborn, R. and Freyberg, P. (1985) *Learning in Science: The Implications of Children's Science*. London: Heinemann.

Selley, N. (1999) *The Art of Constructivist Teaching in the Primary School: A Guide for Students and Teachers*. London: David Fulton.

Whitehead, M. (1997) *Language and Literacy in the Early Years* (2nd edn). London: Chapman.

Personal and Social Development

Curry, M. and Bromfield, C. (1995) *Personal and Social Education for Primary Schools through Circle Time*. Tamworth: Nasen.

Hughes, E. (1994) *Religious Education in the Primary School: Managing Diversity*. London: Cassell.

Millard, A. (1990) *Ideas for Assemblies*. Cambridge: Cambridge University Press.

Swain, S. (1998) *More Christian Assemblies for Primary Schools*. London: SPCK Publishing.

Language and Literacy

Browne, A. (1996) *Developing Language and Literacy 3–8*. London: Chapman.

Marsh, J. and Hallet, E. (eds), (1999) *Desirable Literacies: Approaches to Language and Literacy in the Early Years*. London: Chapman.

Whitehead, M. (1997) *Language and Literacy in the Early Years*. Buckingham: Open University Press.

Mathematics

Thompson, I. (ed.), (1997) *Teaching and Learning Early Number*. Buckingham: Open University Press.

Anghileri, J. (ed.), (1995) *Children's Mathematical Thinking in the Primary Years*. London: Cassell.

Duncan, A. (1996) *What Primary Teachers Should Know about Maths* (2nd edn). London: Hodder and Stoughton.

Haylock, D. and Cockburn, A. (1989) *Understanding Early Years Mathematics*, London: Chapman.

Hughes, M. (1986) *Children and Number*. Oxford: Blackwell.

Jennings, S. and Dunne, R. (1997) *Mathematics for Primary Teachers: An Audit and Self-Study Guide*. London: Letts Educational.

Orton, A. and Frobisher, L. (1996) *Insights into Teaching Mathematics*. London: Cassell.

Knowledge and Understanding of the World

Fran, M. (1995) *Teaching Early Years Geography*. Cambridge: Kington.

Johnsey, R. (1998) *Exploring Primary Design and Technology*. London: Cassell.

National Curriculum Council (1993) *An Introduction to Teaching Geography at Key Stages 1 and 2*. York: NCC.

Ritchie, R. (1995) *Primary Design and Technology: A Process for Learning*. London: David Fulton.

Smart, L. (1995) *Using IT in Primary School History*. London: Cassell.

Wenham, M. (1995) *Understanding Primary Science: Ideas, Concepts and Explanations*. London: Chapman.

Wiegand, P. (1993) *Children and Primary Geography*. London: Cassell.

Wood, L. and Holden C. (1995) *Teaching Early Years History*. Cambridge: Kington.

Physical development and physical education (PE)

Bilton, H. (1998) *Outdoor Play in the Early Years*. London: Fulton.

Department for Education (1995) *Physical Education*. London: HMSO.

Heald, C. (1998) *Physical Development*. Leamington Spa: Scholastic.

Manners, H. K. (1995) *A Framework for Physical Education in the Early Years*. London: Falmer Press.

Wood, E. and Attfield, J. (1996) *Play, Learning and the Early Childhood Curriculum*. London: Chapman.

Creative Development

Gentle, K. (1993) *Teaching Painting in the Primary School*. London: Cassell.

Glover, J. and Ward, S. (eds) (1998) T*eaching Music in the Primary School* (2nd edn). London: Cassell.

Early Information and Communications Technology (ICT)

Crompton, R. and Mann, P. (eds) (1997) *IT Across the Primary Curriculum*. London: Cassell.

Loveless, A. (1995) *The Role of IT: Practical Issues for the Primary Teacher*. London: Cassell.

Griffin, J. and Bash, L. (eds) (1995) *Computeïrs in the Primary School*. London: Cassell.

2

Planning, Teaching and Class Management

SUMMARY

Chapter 1 dealt with the need for 3–8 teachers to have a good knowledge and understanding of the curriculum. However, teachers of 3–8 pupils must also be good planners, managers and communicators. Knowing what needs to be taught is insufficient qualification on its own for being effective as a 3–8 teacher. Such knowledge needs to be underpinned by a practical capability.

Teachers need to be able to

- devise stimulating and interesting activities at an appropriate level for young children;
- offer a broad and balanced curriculum that promotes children's development across a broad front, going beyond the academic to include social, physical and emotional dimensions;
- foster a set of positive attitudes and values;
- manage a class effectively, including the ability to take into account and respond to the needs, abilities and previous experiences (including home experiences) of the children;
- provide opportunities for first-hand experience, discussion and investigation that allow children to utilize all their senses and develop skills and knowledge in a variety of contexts; and
- make the best possible use of the available adults (nursery nurses, parents, other professionals) to support and encourage learning.

By the end of this chapter you should

- know how to plan activities which take account of pupils' needs and their developing physical, intellectual, emotional and social abilities (B4a-e, B5a);
- know how to provide structured learning opportunities which advance pupils' learning across the curriculum (B1, B2, B5bi-v, B5c-g);
- know about the Code of Practice for dealing with children with Special Educational Needs (B4l);
- know about organizing and managing classes and groups of children (B4f-i,k,n);
- know about organizing the learning environment (B4j);
- know about effective teaching methods (B4ki-xiv, B4m); and
- know about managing other adults in the nursery/classroom (B5h).

Planning the 3–8 Curriculum

A U D I T

By the end of this section you should

- understand the need to provide clear structures for lessons, and sequences of lessons, in the short, medium and longer term (B4b);
- be able to plan opportunities that contribute to pupils' wider development (i.e. personal and social) (B4d);
- understand the need to ensure coverage of the Desirable Outcomes/Early Learning Goals and National Curriculum programmes of study (B4e);
- be aware of the need to plan opportunities that will foster concentration and perseverance in young children (B5f).

Why Plan?

Much of children's learning takes place in relatively unstructured contexts outside of the nursery/school, for example, at home or through the media. Teachers, however, are engaged in building on children's previous learning in a more organized fashion, based on the Desirable Outcomes and early learning goals or National Curriculum Programmes of Study. Planning is an essential skill which all teachers must master in order to be able to do this. There are many distractions in 3–8 settings which may deflect teachers from their planning, but without a clear scheme to begin with, these distractions will come to rule. It is very hard as a teacher to think on your feet if you are already thinking on your feet. An absence of effective planning can have serious consequences for teaching and learning. It can lead both to teacher inefficiency and ineffectiveness in the classroom, and to learning that is, at best, patchy and uncoordinated. Lessons and activities that are planned are far more likely to be satisfying and successful than those that are not.

Effective planning

- provides a clear focus and purpose for lessons and schemes of work;
- assists teachers to focus on their own practice, making it easier to reflect on events, modify future teaching, and to anticipate needs and have responses ready;
- is not a straightjacket – paradoxically, it actually allows teachers to be more flexible and to make calculated detours, enabling them to adjust their timing and modify their intentions much more easily; and
- helps teachers to avoid wasting time and missing learning opportunities.

Types of Planning

The School Curriculum and Assessment Authority (SCAA) has identified a number of different levels of planning (SCAA, 1995). The following section gives a brief outline of the progression through long-, medium- and short-term planning and includes examples from nursery/reception and Key Stage 1.

Long-term planning

Long-term planning provides broad frameworks outlining the curriculum to be taught during a child's time in the nursery or school. Long-term planning of this sort ought to reflect the nursery/school policies and the whole staff should be involved in developing and approving the final versions. Long-term plans need to cover the full range of Desirable Outcomes/Early Learning Goals and National Curriculum subject areas, and address coherence, continuity and progression across the various subjects and areas of learning, and between year groups and key stages.

Long-term plans contain

- the content that needs to be covered;
- the organization of that content into manageable and coherent sections;
- identification of any *real* links between the various aspects of the curriculum; and
- the balance between, and time available for, the various subjects and areas of learning.

Long-term planning may also be used by nurseries and schools in areas such as transition into nursery and between nursery and school, induction arrangements for new children, and themes, festivals and visits to be incorporated into the curriculum at various times during the year.

Medium-term planning

Medium-term planning covers the details of the programme to be taught to a particular year group and includes identification of assessment opportunities. Such planning is based on the nursery/school long-term plans. It should involve the whole nursery team or year group team within a school, and is normally comprised of termly or half-termly schemes, showing

- continuing, blocked and linked work (SCAA, 1995); and
- the contexts within which Desirable Outcomes/Early Learning Goals will be developed, for example, in the role-play area or through themes such as 'Materials'.

Medium-term plans will

- outline the learning objectives (based on the Desirable Outcomes/Early Learning Goals or National Curriculum Programmes of Study);
- indicate the resources needed where some form of advance action will be required, such as booking loan materials from libraries and museums;
- suggest teaching methods and ways of organizing the children; and
- include opportunities for assessment.

Short-term planning

This focuses upon daily/weekly teaching and assessment. Short-term planning is derived from medium-term planning but is more specific and detailed, showing

- clear learning purposes;
- key skills, concepts and vocabulary to be introduced or reinforced;
- the nature of any adult intervention;
- how activities are to be differentiated;
- clear progression through the lesson/session from introduction to conclusion;
- the resources that will be needed;
- how and what might be assessed; and
- where feedback to children will be given.

Short-, Medium- and Long-term Planning

The diagram below shows the relation between the example teaching plans which follow on pages 57–63. The shaded areas are intended to help the reader track particular learning objectives through the process from scheme of work to lesson plan.

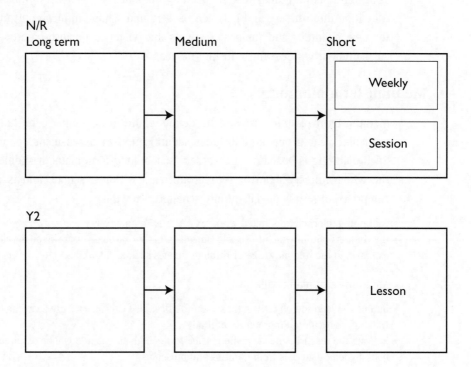

Section from long-term planning – Nursery/Reception
Language and literacy (speaking and listening)

Learning purposes/links to desirable outcomes	Activities	Resourcing	Organization/ management
To extend children's vocabulary	Repeating/reinforcing vocabulary and introducing new words through • 1:1 conversations • intervention in pupil activities • songs and rhymes	Bilingual support staff	With • groups • pairs • individuals
To develop children's confidence and fluency in using: • existing vocabulary • new vocabulary	Set up imaginary (small-scale) play opportunities to promote range and fluency. Themes could include • the garage • the airport • the zoo • the farm	Small-scale play materials: • toy vehicles • animal/human figures • dolls • floor maps • natural materials and other 'scenery'	Through • support during activities • intervention (high, medium and low) • pupil initiated tasks
To develop children's ability to use oral language for a range of purposes: • initiating conversations with adults • making their needs known • initiating conversations with peers • recalling experiences • predicting	Adults to respond in a positive and friendly manner to pupil enquiries Adults to use a wide range of questions about the children's experiences: • who? • what? • when? • where? • how? • why? • what if? • what next?	Exploratory play materials: • sand • water • outdoor	With • groups • pairs • individuals Through • support during activities • intervention (high, medium and low) • pupil initiated tasks

Section from medium-term planning – Nursery/Reception
Half-term 1   Theme – Materials   Area of learning – Language and literacy

Learning purpose(s)/ links to desirable outcomes	Monitoring/ assessment	Indicative activities	Resources	Links to other areas of learning
Week 1 Children will improve their listening skills and initiate conversations with others.	Children can interact in a group situation, knowing when to talk and when to listen. Children can share information and talk about their experiences.	Listening to and discussing talking books and taped stories. Making own taped stories. Newsagent role play area, including newspapers, magazines cards etc. Circle games	Role play material. Computer + talking books. Tape recorder and tapes.	Role play and personal and social development. ICT.
Week 2 Children will develop their ability to explain. Children will express themselves with increasing confidence and fluency.	Children can identify and use new words accurately.	Sand and water play. Walk around the locality. Looking at the properties of materials e.g. rough, smooth, heavy, light.	Sand and water equipment. Display a wide range of different papers and other materials.	Knowledge and understanding of the world.
Week 3 Children will increase their knowledge of books: • structure • types.	Children can identify different types of book e.g. fiction, non-fiction. Children can identify different parts of a book.	Shared reading area featuring fiction, non-fiction, and 'feely' books. Making own paper books in the art area. Using 'own' books to tell stories to others.	Books from library loan service. Pre-prepared 'blank' books in art area.	
Week 4 Children will learn to recognize and reproduce letters.	Children can recognize an increasing number of letters. Children can write their names.	Copying and feeling textured letters. Playing with and drawing 3D letters. Making and decorating name badges in mark-making area. Drawing letters on the computer 'Splosh'.	Letters (plastic, card, wood, etc.). Computer and drawing package.	Creative development.
Week 5 Children will learn that some words rhyme with others.	Children can associate patterns with rhymes. Children can differentiate between rhymes and non-rhymes.	Rhyming names in registration/group times. Recorded rhymes on tape, e.g. plastic and elastic. Card games with rhyming words.	Tape recorder and tapes. Rhyming cards.	Personal and social development.

Section from short-term planning – Nursery/Reception
Half-term 1 – Week 2, weekly planner

Linked/Block work Theme – Materials	Learning purposes	Monday	Tuesday	Wednesday	Thursday	Friday
Language and literacy	Children will develop their ability to • express themselves with increasing confidence and fluency. • identify and use new words accurately.	Work with properties cards (e.g. soft, dull, rough) Learn/practise vocabulary	Sand play Small play apparatus. Animals in the desert.	Walk around the locality. Focus on different materials and new words. Look for use of paper and card in the locality.	Making paper books in writing area.	Opposites game – matching property words to materials (e.g. hard, soft, rough/smooth, heavy/light)
Knowledge and understanding of the world	The children will learn about the similarities and differences between the properties of materials. The children will learn to classify materials according to simple properties (e.g. hard and soft).	Water play Which materials will float/which materials sink?	Food activity. Making playdough food items. Baking and then painting them. Discussing changes to the material.	As above	Handling and describing different papers. Looking for similarities and differences. Deciding which papers to use for covers/pages in book making.	Looking at the properties of other materials (e.g. glass, plastic, stone, metal) on the investigative table.

Continuing/on-going work	Learning purposes	Monday	Tuesday	Wednesday	Thursday	Friday
Personal and social development						
Language and literacy						
Mathematics						
Knowledge and understanding of the world						
Physical development (inc. outdoor play)						
Creative development						
Construction area						
Home corner/ role-play area						
Small play						

Session planner

Date	Learning objective
Thursday, 16 September	Practise existing vocabulary and learn new words related to properties of materials (paper and card)
Assessment	**Links to Desirable Outcomes**
• can use new words accurately when explaining, describing and playing	Language and literacy Knowledge and understanding of the world
Context	**Resources**
Outdoor area, investigative/writing tables	Range of paper and card offcuts, paper/card artefacts (e.g. boxes, books, envelopes) Pens, pencils, scissors, stapler Pre-cut card covers Pre-cut paper pages

Introduction	Discuss previous day's local walk. Reminders about paper and card.

Development (What will the children do?)	**Teaching points (What will the teacher do?)**
Handling and describing paper, card and artefacts Looking at books (paper back, hard back, pop-up etc.). Talking about common features and how the materials have been used (i.e. card covers, paper pages) Making a book of their favourite story, illustrating and writing the text	Introduce/reinforce vocabulary (paper, card, thin, thick, stiff, bendy) Discuss materials and organization of books (cover, page, spine) Assist children in manipulating materials and tools Introduce/reinforce vocabulary (fold, bend, staple, draw, write)
Recap and reinforcement	**Extension/links**
Place books in reading area Ask children to read their story Ask children to describe how they made their book	Friday investigation and describing properties of other materials (wood, plastic)

Learning purposes/links to National Curriculum programmes of study	Activities	Organization/ management	Resources
Life processes and living things (3a–c) • *Plants need light and water to grow.* • *Recognizing and naming parts of flowering plants.* • *Learning that plants produce seeds which in turn produce new plants.* *(5a–b)* • *Learning about different plants and animals in the locality.* • *Learning about different environments locally and that these affect the plants and animals in them.*			
Materials and their properties (2a–b) • *Learning that materials can be changed in shape by squashing, bending, twisting and stretching.* • *Describing how everyday materials change when heated or cooled.*			
Physical processes (2a–d) • *Describing the movements of familiar things.* • *Learning that pushes and pulls are forces.* • *Learning that forces can speed things up, slow down or change direction.* • *Learning that forces can change the shape of objects.*	*Testing wheeled vehicles on ramps* *Balloon power* *Parachutes* *Paper planes* *Stretching threads and strings* *Tug of war/seesaws* *Sailboats* *Friction tests*	*With* • *groups* • *pairs* • *individuals*	*Balloons* *PE beam* *Sturdy rope* *Range of different surfaces (polished to coarse)* *Toy vehicles*
Experimental and investigative science • *Responding to suggestions of how to find things out.* • *Using simple equipment appropriately.* • *Making observations.* • *Comparing objects, living things and events.* • *Describing and recording observations.* • *Using simple tables where appropriate.*			

Section from medium-term planning
Science, Year 2, Half-term 4   Theme – Movement (Physical processes)

Learning purpose(s)	Assessment/ monitoring	Activities/ organization	Resources	Links across the curriculum (including literacy, numeracy and ICT)
Children will describe movement of different objects.	Children can compare the movement of different objects in terms of speed and direction. Children can link the idea of a force to a change on movement.	Rolling toy vehicles down ramps. Measuring distance travelled. Measuring time taken. Altering ramp angles. (Groups)	Toy cars Planks/ramps Stop watches/timers Metre sticks	Maths/numeracy – measuring, recording using simple table
Children will learn that pushes and pulls are both forces.	Children can describe the similarities and differences between pushes and pulls.	Tug of war in playground/hall. Altering size/number of children pulling on each end. Using PE beam to create see-saw. Lifting chldren by pushing down on the lever. (Class)	Sturdy tow rope PE mats Beam and pivot	
Children will learn that forces can make things speed up.	Children can compare the movement of different objects in terms of speed and direction. Children can link the idea of a force to a change on movement.	Jet power. Different sized/shaped balloons attached to drinking straw. String threaded through straw. Measuring speed and distance. Altering angle of string. (Groups)	Balloons Straws String Stop watches/timers Metre sticks	English/literacy (Speaking and listening) – making tape recorded accounts of the investigation and its results.
Children will learn that forces can make things slow down.	Children can compare the movement of different objects in terms of speed and direction. Children can link the idea of a force to a change on movement.	Parachute activity. Lower metal washers to the ground in a controlled fashion using parachutes. Measuring the time taken/number of washers supported. (Class)	Metal washers Plastic bin liners Range of alternative sheet materials (paper, thin textiles) String Stop watches/timers Metre sticks Parents/non-teaching support	ICT – Using word processing package to write about the activity.
Children will learn that forces can change the shape of objects/materials.	Children can compare the effects of forces on the shape of different objects/ materials (i.e. more force = more change).	Clay work. (Groups)	Boards Water pots Range of objects with which to apply a force including clay tools.	

Section from short-term planning
Science, Year 2, Half-term 1 – Week 3   Lesson plan

Session – *Parachutes*

Learning purpose(s)

Children will learn that forces can make things slow down

Resources

Metal washers, Plastic bin liners
Range of alternative sheet materials (paper, thin textiles)
String, Stop watches/timers, Metre sticks, Recording sheets

Teaching points

- *Outline purpose and activity*
- *Drop objects from different heights into sand tray. Talk to children about how and why the objects fall.*
- *Ask children to think of ways that the objects could be slowed down.*
- *Demonstrate operation of a parachute to class.*
- *Seek explanations; focus on air pushing up while gravity pulls down.*
- *Ask for suggestions for fair testing e.g. same size parachute, same number of washers, same shaped parachutes, same materials used, same height of drop.*
- *Ask children to return to tables and begin making their parachutes.*
- *Test parachutes by dropping from a chair, 1 child to drop, 1 to oversee fair testing, 1 to record results.*
- *Ask children to return materials and equipment and then to sit in the carpet area.*

Class – *Y2*

Assessment opportunities

Children can compare the movement of different objects in terms of speed and direction.
Children can link the idea of a force to a change of movement.

Date – *21/3/00*   **Time** – *p.m.*

Pupil activities

As a class
- *Observing demonstration, asking and answering questions*
- *Suggesting ways of fair testing*

Working in threes
- *Using simple equipment appropriately*
- *Making observations*
- *Comparing events*
- *Describing and recording observations.*

Clearing work areas and returning to carpet.

Differentiation/extension tasks

- *Pre-cut parachutes for children struggling to use scissors accurately*
- *Using different sized parachutes/different materials/different shapes and comparing results for quick finishers*

Plenary

- *Recap, reinforce and check on children's learning about air resistance and gravity as examples of pushes and pulls*
- *Show children 'egg on a chute'. Don't tell them it's hard boiled!*
- *Ask for predictions*
- *Test*

Lessons need clear objectives or learning purposes which indicate what the children are going to learn or practise. Sharing these learning purposes with the children can help them to achieve the intended outcomes. There may be many possible activities that would allow children to achieve a particular learning objective; trainee and newly qualified teachers need to be clear about the distinction between the purposes of a lesson and the activity that the children will do. Learning purposes moreover, should not be too numerous. It is both inappropriate and unreasonable to expect children in this age group to achieve large numbers of teaching objectives in any one lesson or session.

In addition to learning purposes, teachers also need criteria by which to assess the children's achievements. How will you know if the purpose of the lesson or session has been met? In order to answer this question, it is necessary to identify what a child must do to demonstrate achievement. For 5–8 pupils, these criteria for assessment can be drawn from National Literacy Strategy statements, National Numeracy Strategy statements and from National Curriculum level descriptions. These will be dealt with in more detail in Chapter 3.

Planning for the youngest children

For those working with the youngest children, planning ought to be informed by an understanding of the ways in which these pupils learn. Young children develop and grow rapidly. They learn well in situations and circumstances that are real and relevant to their lives, and through activities that are varied and interesting. While they will follow recognized patterns of development during this period, individuals vary considerably. Cognitive development may not necessarily be a smooth and continuous process; it may even be susceptible to regression. Children arrive in nursery and reception classes from a wide variety of backgrounds, with a broad range of experiences, and at different stages of development. Their experiences in 3–5 settings constitue a key stage in their learning and development.

Planning for nursery/reception children

- Build upon the children's previous (home) experiences and learning.
- Recognize that young children's needs and interests will grow and develop over time.
- Offer opportunities for children to explore significant events in their lives and encourage self-expression and discovery.
- Capitalize on the valuable lessons to be learned through the wider curriculum such as conventions relating to health and safety, playing sensibly in the playground, behaviour both in the nursery/school and on outside visits, and involvement in events and productions such as festivals, concerts and celebrations.

Young children are inquisitive and many everyday occurrences capture their imagination and provoke demands for explanations. Nursery/reception programmes attempt to make this natural desire to find out, and the children's natural ability to soak up information, work for them by providing a curriculum with opportunities for inquiry. Planning includes opportunities for children to handle a range of tools and materials, to observe, listen, investigate, question, experiment and draw conclusions. This inquiry element is supported by teachers who

- help the children make links between previous experiences and current discoveries and establish an environment in which the children feel safe, secure and confident; and
- ensure a balance between teacher-initiated tasks (i.e. where the teacher is guiding the children's learning) and child-initiated activities (i.e. those activities selected by a child on the basis of their personal interests and abilities).

While teacher accountability and national documentation may require teachers to think about and plan the curriculum in terms of subject areas, young children do not automatically make the same distinctions. The under-5s' curriculum provides a coherent framework for addressing the various discrete areas of learning while at the same time offering teachers and children opportunities to make links between these various areas of learning. For example, visiting the local shops with the children can offer starting points and opportunities for learning in language and literacy, mathematics, personal and social development, and health education.

Planning to address the different areas of learning in 3–5 settings

Personal and social development
Your planning should include opportunities for children to
- become more self-confident; to express themselves and articulate their interests, preferences, thoughts and ideas;
- share their experiences with their peers and adults, identifying and recognizing their achievements and strengths, including perseverance and self-control;
- demonstrate concern for others, (for example, helping to clean up, or looking after someone in the playground);
- share resources with others;
- become more self-reliant, (for example, by encouraging them to learn their address and telephone number, to become increasingly proficient in dressing themselves after PE, and to make decisions about their work, such as when and where to seek help and support); and
- become more responsible, (for example, by observing conventions and routines in the nursery/classroom such as following basic safety rules).

Language and literacy
Your planning should include opportunities for children to
- develop their speaking and listening skills through
    listening and responding to stories and rhymes;
    showing their understanding of stories by predicting outcomes;
    responding appropriately to questions;

65

repeating words;

naming letter characters and sounds;

following simple directions;

describing personal experiences and retelling familiar stories;

• develop their reading and writing skills through

identifying signs and labels;

learning names;

imitating writing;

using gestures and tone of voice to communicate meaning more effectively;

showing awareness of the conventions of written material (left to right, spaces between words, upper and lower case letters);

identifing key features of books (title, pictures);

using key features to understand and tell stories;

contributing words and sentences to a narrative scribed by the teacher;

writing simple messages (printing letters in the alphabet, writing their own names and familiar names, and simple words such as 'dog' and 'cat').

Mathematics

Your planning should include opportunities for children to

• increase their mathematical understanding through

demonstrating their understanding of whole numbers;

measuring (i.e. comparing length, weight, mass, capacity and awareness of time);

identifying characteristics of simple two- and three-dimensional shapes;

recognizing and using patterns;

collecting, showing and understanding simple data;

seeking clarification, help and equipment when needed);

Knowledge and understanding of the world

Your planning should include opportunities for children to

• show curiosity and enthusiasm for investigating and exploring;

• demonstrate awareness and concern for living things and the environment;

• learn about the properties of familiar materials;

• take some responsibility for planning and organizing their work with support; and

• become familiar with technology (including ICT)

Physical development

Your planning should include opportunities for children to

• practice personal hygiene;

• show awareness of safe and unsafe situations and resources (sharp scissors, large apparatus);

• participate in regular physical activity including dance and movement;

• use a wide range of large and small apparatus to develop gross and fine motor control (bicycles, climbing frames, barrels, balls, crayons, paint brushes, scissors); and

• improve their balance, agility and spatial awareness (running and jumping, using scooters and other riding toys, using climbing frames).

Creative development

Your planning should include opportunities for children to

• express their thoughts and feelings using a wide range of media;

- experiment with and investigate tools, techniques and materials;
- perform (using puppet theatres, making music, dancing);
- learn songs and rhymes;
- enact and reenact stories in the structured play area;
- respond appropriately to the tempo and mood of music (fast, slow, scary, happy); and
- learn about the visual arts (colour, shape and size).

Individual Pupil Needs and Abilities

AUDIT

By the end of this section you should

- understand how to match learning objectives and content to the needs and abilities of pupils (B4ai);
- be aware of the importance of challenging children and having appropriate expectations for children's learning (B4aii, B4aiii);
- understand the need to build on prior attainment, and to share the content and purposes of lessons and activities with the children (B4aiv).

Young children can learn in different ways, at different speeds, can experience a variety of different learning difficulties, and can reach very different levels of attainment. Many teachers would agree that diversity exists in their classes. Teacher responses to individual pupil needs and abilities include: organizational, such as ability grouping; differentiating the curriculum when planning and teaching; and tailoring expectations according to the pupils' needs and abilities.

Differentiating – matching tasks to children's abilities – is not a new idea for 3–8 teachers. Long before the introduction of the National Curriculum, Desirable Outcomes or Early Learning Goals, authors concerned with good nursery and primary practice were referring to the need for teachers to think about the children's abilities, previous experience, interests, knowledge and skills, as well as paying attention to the subject matter and the range of teaching styles and methods (Dean, 1985).

Children vary: from each other; from day to day; from year to year; in their abilities; in their behaviour; and in their attitudes.

Differentiation is an important element in effective teaching and learning in order to 'maximise the motivation, progress and achievement of each student' (Stradling and Saunders, 1993).

Differentiation should result in the provision of tasks which will enable children to

- consolidate their existing understanding;
- practise their existing skills;
- build on such understanding and skills;
- encounter and master new ideas and enlarge their knowledge of a subject; and
- engage in creative and imaginative thinking and action. (Alexander *et al.*, 1992)

A key factor to consider when differentiating is that ability is not necessarily *universal* or *fixed*. A pupil's ability may well alter over time and could depend on the subject matter. The notion that children have habitual levels of achievement is supported by common sense and anecdotal evidence rather than by hard facts (SCAA, 1994). It is entirely possible that achievement is domain specific rather than universal, and is unstable rather than fixed (SCAA, 1994, p. 26, 5.1.3., para. 3). In addition, the domains in question may not be different subjects, such as English and art, but could quite easily be between aspects of the same subject such as writing and reading (for example, children who can read words that they cannot yet spell).

Universal ability: a child's ability is the same across the whole curriculum
Fixed ability: a child's ability relative to his/her peers will not alter over time
Domain specific ability: a child performs better in some areas of the curriculum than in others
Unstable ability: a child's ability can improve and regress.

Howard Gardner (Cotton, 1995) has suggested that people possess a range of intelligences and that some may be much more highly developed than others. In formal education the emphasis is often on linguistic and mathematical intelligences; however, Gardner's research identified seven different types of intelligence. Awareness of these intelligences can help teachers to appreciate more fully the strengths and potential that children may have.

Gardner's seven types of intelligence
- Linguistic: the ability to use words (orally or in writing) effectively;
- Mathematical (logical): the ability to use reason and numbers effectively;
- Visual (spatial): the ability to visualize the world around you accurately, to represent things visually and to manipulate images mentally;
- Musical: the ability to identify clearly, change and express music;
- Bodily (kinaesthetic): the ability to use your body and/or hands to express ideas and make or change objects;
- Interpersonal: the ability to be sensitive to the emotions and thoughts of other people;
- Intrapersonal: the ability to be reflective and understand one's own strengths and weaknesses.

Given that ability may be domain specific and unstable, those working in 3–8 settings need to start from the premise that every child is good at something, and success in one area can breed success and increased confidence in other areas. A second strategy is to retain a degree of flexibility and to be prepared to try a range of different approaches, including differentiation by support, differentiation by outcome and differentiation by task.

68

Differentiation by Support

Although the difficulties involved in differentiating should not be underestimated, much of what is already common practice in nurseries and classrooms can make a contribution to the task. Most teachers already adapt, alter and adjust the demands placed on children during teaching and learning in order to support or extend particular individuals or groups. Differentiation of this sort implies a variation in the level of teacher intervention provided and in the level of autonomy offered to children. This can have implications for the organization and management of lessons and activities, as it is often the case that the dialogue and interaction between teachers and individual children is less than it might be, and is often concentrated at the start and conclusion of sessions.

While there are individual differences between children, there are also similarities and common needs. These similarities can make differentiation through teacher support more manageable, as matching tasks to pupils may involve consideration of groups and classes as well as individuals. Appreciating the differences between children in this more general fashion can be helpful to trainee and newly qualified teachers as a starting point when beginning to decide on which approach to differentiation might work, in which context and with which children.

Differentiating through teacher support

- Alter the amount, range and complexity of sources of information.
- Structure a task tightly for some children while allowing others more room to plan, organize and manage themselves.
- Identify those children likely to struggle and plan ways of assisting them to cope with the demands of the lesson or session.
- Identify those children likely to find the task easy and plan ways of making the task more demanding to ensure they are suitably challenged.

Differentiation by Outcome and Task

The terms differentiation by outcome and differentation by task have been useful in getting teachers to focus on the issue of differentiation and to hone their practice. However, they ought to be seen as a starting point for understanding how to differentiate and not as providing the definitive description of how to ensure appropriate and demanding expectations of children.

Differentiation by outcome

This involves pupils undertaking the same task while working at their own level. While this will always be a useful option, differentiation by outcome should not be used as an excuse for not considering differentiation at all, or in other words, differentiation by accident.

When teachers differentiate by outcome they recognize the implications:

1. Activities and materials should be equally accessible to all children and ought not to be dependent upon knowledge and skills which only some of the children have.
2. There should be a range of possible answers and outcomes. Ultimately, if a task is to be truly defined as differentiated by outcome it needs to offer all the children involved the chance to make progress.

Differentiation by task

This may take a number of forms, including:
1. Children covering the same content but at different levels.
2. Children covering the same content but with different activities.
3. Children covering the same content, activity and level, but being taught using different approaches.

When differentiating by task teachers need to remember that children have an entitlement to certain skills and knowledge within the National Curriculum and Desirable Outcomes/Early Learning Goals. In order to ensure that differentiation by task and the entitlement curriculum are compatible, a distinction needs to be drawn between between the purpose of an activity and the way in which that purpose is addressed. For example, if teachers need children to learn 'addition and subtraction facts to 20' (DFE, 1995) there are many ways in which they can set about achieving this.

Deciding how to Differentiate

It is sometimes hard to say with any certainty where one form of differentiation ends and another begins, particularly as different approaches could be employed at different points within the same lesson or activity. A task might be identified as differentiated by outcome on the surface, yet within that the teacher may use a range of different techniques (including challenges, questions and procedures) for different individuals and groups.

A design and technology class activity

Here is an example is of a design and technology activity for a class of Y2 infants based on a visit to the local playground. The teacher's primary purpose is to teach the pupils to 'measure, mark out, cut and shape a range of materials' (DfEE, 1995, p. 58, D+T PoS4b).

Differentiation by outcome

- When *clarifying the task* the children talked about their visit to the site and were then told that they would be designing a piece of playground apparatus. The teacher discussed the features of apparatus with the children and they decided that all the products should be fun to use and safe.

- The children were asked to *design* their apparatus in pairs using pencil and paper.

- When *making* their playground models the teacher put out a limited selection of tools and materials (including hacksaws, benchhooks, square section softwood, cardboard, PVA adhesive, string, and scissors) to which all the children had access.

- When *evaluating* their models the children all used the original criteria of fun and safety.

Differentiation by task

- *Clarifying the task.* Following the visit, some children were asked to respond to the broad question 'What would make an exciting piece of playground equipment?' Others were asked to respond to much more specific queries such as 'What should our climbing frame be like?' The teacher assisted and guided one group of children closely as they began to identify criteria and specifications arising from the answers to the second question. The first group was expected to operate more independently and to make a written list in pairs.

- *Designing.* Some of the children designed their models informally and prior to making them. Most of the class drew their designs. Three very able children were asked to produce two alternative designs and select the best.

- *Making.* Different children were provided with different materials and equipment. For the majority of the class this meant scissors, paper and card, straws, soft wood and hacksaws. One group, which was proceeding rapidly and effectively, was offered additional tools and materials to produce their final product. One group was asked to construct their climbing frame using a commercially produced construction kit.

- *Evaluation.* When engaged in critical reflection and evaluation of their work some children used a worksheet, while a small group who had difficulty with writing discussed their views with the teacher acting as scribe. The teacher employed different types of questions with different children including procedural questions such as 'How are you going to do that?', questions about outcomes such as 'Have you done what you set out to do?' and questions about understanding, such as 'How does it work?' and 'How could you make it work better?'

The ability to differentiate tasks for children, based on judgements about their needs and abilities, plays an important role in helping children to achieve in any subject or area of learning. However, the realities of nursery and primary classrooms make these things 'aspirations rather than absolutes' (Alexander *et al.*, 1992, p. 28). Differentiation is a demanding task for teachers, one that is made even more difficult in situations where

- teachers experience a lack of access to support from other adults (curriculum coordinators, CCAs, NTAs, parents);
- resources are limited or not available; and
- class sizes are large and the available space is insufficient.

The checklist below can be used by trainee and newly qualified teachers when attempting to overcome the demands of differentiating in their planning and teaching.

Differentiation checklist

- Monitor your teaching materials to ensure that they support, extend and allow for achievement by all the children.
- Adjust the degree of independence and responsibility for organizing and running tasks and activities.
- Use a wide range of recording methods.
- Recognize the successes of all pupils and challenge them to extend their knowledge and skills.
- Organize the nursery/classroom to support group work and collaborative learning as well as class and individual teaching.
- Monitor children's experiences, target your time and attention towards certain children at certain points, and alter the intensity of teacher intervention between levels that could be described as high, medium, or low.
- Undertake formative assessment and enter into dialogue with pupils as a way of setting new targets and identifying learning difficulties.
- Make effective use of other adults and support staff in the classroom, including parents, NTAs and visitors.

Children with Special Educational Needs (SEN)

By the end of this section you should

- be familiar with some of the characteristics displayed by children who have special educational needs (B4av);
- be familiar with the teacher's responsibilities under the Code of Practice on the identification and assessment of special educational needs (B4l).

Teachers of young children play an important part in identifying and assessing children with special educational needs. Such assessments may involve consultation and collaboration with external agencies to discuss and plan learning programmes aimed at meeting their specific needs. The teacher's role in tackling SEN includes

- providing support to enable children to have equal access to the curriculum; and
- providing opportunities for appropriate learning experiences, including social ones.

It has been estimated that as many as one in five children will have some form of special educational need at some point during their school lives (Dearing, 1993). Such special educational needs might involve social, emotional, physical and intellectual factors. Special educational needs are considered to exist in circumstances or situations where special provision has to be made for a child because they are either very able or are experiencing difficulty. SEN pupils may be struggling or they could be particularly gifted and talented. Where the need is based on a difficulty, rather than on a particular gift or talent, this can range from mild to severe. A learning difficulty in the context of SEN implies a significantly greater difficulty in learning than that experienced by the majority of children of the same age. In addition, a special educational need might be the result of a disability which precludes or hampers children's efforts to avail themselves of educational facilities. Examples of such disabilities include

- visual or hearing impairment;
- physical or neurological impairment;
- speech and language difficulties; and
- emotional and behavioural difficulties.

Efforts to support young children with SEN can be greatly aided by positive relationships with parents and carers. Parental involvement can be highly effective in assisting children to overcome cognitive, linguistic, behavioural or emotional difficulties. Parents and carers should be included and involved in the decision-making concerning their child and be encouraged to contribute and support their child's development in partnership with the nursery or school. Where such involvement is encouraged, parents are more likely to have a positive attitude towards the process and their child. Where such involvement is not encouraged, parents may feel threatened or criticised and may be reluctant both to accept that a problem exists and to support the efforts of professionals to help their child overcome difficulties.

Involving parents and carers

- Listen to what parents have to say.
- Include parents and carers at an early stage.
- Demonstrate an understanding of, and respect for, the feelings of parents and carers.
- Make every effort to maintain good channels of communication so that children's progress can be reported.

Recognizing Children with SEN

Very able children are often capable of pursuing their learning in greater depth and at a faster pace than their peers. Differentiation is essential for these children because it makes the curriculum more complex and demanding. Children who have a learning difficulty will have very different needs from their more able peers. Differentiation can provide ways of allowing these children to pursue their work at a more appropriate pace.

Markers to watch for

Children who are very able in a particular subject or area of learning may
- display a good memory for facts, people or events;
- possess good powers of observation;
- like to know how things work or happen;
- be able to follow relatively complex instructions;
- have a wide vocabulary which they use accurately;
- possess good physical coordination and control;
- have a high level of visual and spatial awareness;
- display a high degree of independence, self-sufficiency and initiative;
- be ambitious, setting themselves high goals;
- display good social skills with older children and adults, and have a well-developed sense of humour. At the same time they may experience difficulties with their peers, dominating others if allowed to do so, and attempting to monopolize the teacher.
(OFSTED, 1993)

Children who are experiencing learning difficulties in a particular subject or area of learning may
- find it hard to understand the language used;
- have a limited concentration span and appear to indulge in apparent time-wasting or work avoidance;
- experience problems in transferring and applying knowledge and skills;

- exhibit poor general knowledge;
- find following instructions difficult; and
- display a lack of care and attention when working and a propensity for losing things.

In both cases, and wherever SEN are thought to exist, teachers of 3–8 pupils need to be familiar with the Code of Practice for addressing these needs.

Code of Practice for Special Educational Needs

SEN may be identified when a child starts school or nursery. Concern over a child's progress can be registered at this point by teachers, parents, other carers or external agencies. Concerns may also arise at any time during the nursery and school years. Whenever there appears to be cause for concern, the nursery/school SEN coordinator needs to be involved, as do the parents or carers.

Following the Code of Practice

The class teacher will take the lead in gathering information and evidence and completing an **initial cause for concern** sheet. Depending on the nature of the cause for concern, teaching staff may also need to seek information from others. For example, when a teacher suspects that a child has behavioural problems, they may need to establish a more accurate picture by talking to parents, carers or lunchtime supervisors.

Following the initial cause for concern, teachers are required to **monitor** the child over a period of time and maintain a record of progress at intervals. Notes and observations need to be carefully collated and dated since they will be shared with and communicated to parents, carers, the SEN coordinator and possibly external agencies.

If, after a half-term's monitoring, the child seems not to have made any progress, the teacher must complete a **Stage One** action form and continue the monitoring.

If, following two Stage One reviews, there still does not appear to be any progress, teachers must complete a **Stage Two** action form which results in the setting up of an **individual education programme** (IEP) which must be reviewed on a termly basis. The IEP will describe the nature of the child's difficulties and will outline the action(s) to be taken. In some cases the action will involve special provision and may include learning support either from outside agencies or from SEN staff employed by the nursery/school. For the majority of children, early identification and appropriate intervention leads to them overcoming their difficulties. It is possible that a review of the Code of Practice will result in a conflation of Stages 1 and 2.

If the IEP does not result in progress, the decision must be made to move to **Stage Three** –seeking formal assistance from external agencies.

Having involved the external agencies it may become apparent that the existing provision available to the child is inappropriate or insufficient to help them overcome their difficulties in which case the decision is made to move to **Stage Four**. Stage Four involves a more formal assessment of the child's needs and will result in a formal **Statement of Special Educational Needs**. At this point the local education authority takes responsibility for overseeing and managing the task of addressing the child's needs, albeit still in consultation and collaboration with parents/carers and the school. The issuing of a Statement of Special Educational Needs carries with it the mandatory requirement to conduct an annual review.

Stage Five is at the top of the scale. Children on Stage Five of the special needs register are entitled by law to even greater levels of special provision. For example, children with severe physical and learning difficulties will have support workers who accompany them throughout the school day.

Working with the Code of Practice

John, a Y1 pupil, was deemed to have moderate learning difficulties and was at Stage Two under the Code of Practice. It was suspected that he was struggling with an attention deficiency disorder. He was easily distracted during lessons. His poor concentration and attention resulted in him wandering off task and interfering with other children which often resulted in squabbles. He also had unrealistic expectations of his abilities, leading to frustration and a tendency to give up quickly. His teacher therefore tried to plan work for John that was short and focused. In addition she made sure that John understood the purposes of the sessions and the likely outcomes and made sure too that he received plenty of praise and recognition for his efforts. During literacy hour sessions, John would work with a special needs support teacher who provided short focused tasks on phonics and reading. John was encouraged to reflect and comment on his own learning and progress as a way of raising his self-esteem and modifying his behaviour by promoting his ability to persevere.

Organizing the Children and Class Management

By the end of this section you should

- understand how to make effective use of teaching time in whole class and group situations (B4f);
- be aware of the link between classroom organization, sound learning and good behaviour (B4g);
- be familiar with strategies for establishing a purposeful working atmosphere in whole-class and group situations (B4h);
- be familiar with strategies for establishing and maintaining a good standard of behaviour, well-focused teaching, and positive and productive relationships in whole-class and group situations (B4i).

This section is based on the premise that strategies such as class teaching and groupwork are not inherently good or bad but are simply options open to teachers who have to make choices about the best way to organize and manage a particular lesson or session. Teachers should group children on the basis of *fitness for purpose* rather than on the basis of dogmatic adherence to traditional practice.

Teaching classes

Young children have always experienced some form of class teaching whether at morning registration, at story time, in PE or in dance and movement. As a method of organizing the children for learning, it has become increasingly common in infant schools, particularly with the advent of literacy and numeracy hours. Alexander *et al.*, (1992, Section 4, p. 23, paras 89–92) made a strong case for seeing class teaching as an essential part of the teacher's repertoire, placing the onus on them to be an organizer, giver of information, leader and the focus of attention.

Benefits and disadvantages associated with class teaching

Benefits	**Disadvantages**
• higher order questioning	• too much teacher talk
• more detailed explanations	• an absence of active learning by children
• 'higher levels of pupil performance'	• individual differences ignored
(Alexander *et al.*, 1992)	

When working with a large number of young children, trainee and newly qualified teachers need to bear in mind the age and maturity of these learners. Teachers who keep young pupils sitting passively for too long are asking for trouble. So too are teachers who do not check that their instructions have been understood before setting the children to work. The following suggestions are intended to assist trainee and newly qualified teachers to organize the children and manage class situations.

Managing a whole class

• Ensure that the necessary resources are set out or readily available.
• Think about the language and vocabulary that you will use.
• Obtain and maintain the children's attention. Waiting for silence can be done *actively* through effective use of the voice and non-verbal communication. Having something interesting to show can be highly effective as a technique for getting little eyes, ears and minds all pointed in the right direction. A teacher whose whole body says 'Look at me! This is going to be really interesting' is more likely to gain the children's attention, and gaining this attention is crucial if you are to create a *window of opportunity*.
• Do not squander the chance to start the lesson well. A prompt start, followed by an appropriate, yet business-like pace will help to avoid the creation of deadtime and set the tone for the lesson.

- Pacing and timing are crucial. Some children may be left floundering if the pace is too rapid. Others may lose their concentration and enthusiasm if the pace is too languid; they may start fiddling or interrupting. You can lose the initiative and spend unnecessary amounts of time trying to regain their attention.
- Finishing class lessons in an organized fashion is every bit as important as starting them well. It is part of the learning process, providing opportunities for review and reflection and giving you a chance to ascertain the extent of the children's experiences and learning.

- Being overtaken by time is often a problem for trainee and newly qualified teachers when teaching the whole class. Allow time for plenary sessions and putting things away. Learning to put things away properly is a long-term process with young children, and requires determination and consistency on the teacher's part. Encourage children to take some responsibility for tidying up and looking after their learning environment; a shared classroom ethos in which the children have had an opportunity to decide that 'In our class we always . . .' will help.

Groupwork

A significant amount of teaching with the 3–8 age range takes place using groupwork. Groupwork involves small numbers of children working collaboratively on a task and should not be confused with situations where the setting is collaborative (i.e. children sitting in groups) but the pupils are engaged in individual learning tasks (Alexander *et al.*, (1992) Section 4, paras 93–8).

Benefits and disadvantages of groupwork

Benefits
- encourages pupil–pupil interaction
- promotes communication and cooperation
- encourages children to take more responsibility for their own learning, setting the pace, asking questions, and developing answers
- promotes participation, high involvement and commitment

Disadvantages
- can be quite slow
- the positive social dynamics of groupwork are not automatic and can require input from the teacher
- can be difficult to manage several groups

Some groupwork options

- Grouping for learning, (on the basis of ability or needs) can be a very effective and efficient way of teaching. However, if the groups are permanent two problems can arise. First, children pick up unspoken messages about their ranking and status in the classroom; they soon know that the 'red group' is the 'top' group. For those children who see themselves as less able this can have an adverse effect on their self-esteem and motivation. Second, teachers themselves can be affected in that their expectations can be coloured by their own groupings, leading to under- and over-estimating ability.

- Some teachers will seek to group children by age/maturity. This is frequently the case in vertically grouped classes (Y1 and Y2 together) that often appear where school numbers dictate.
- Grouping by friendship can be a powerful motivator for children but there are dangers. Single sex groups may appear where you would prefer mixed sex groups. There can be children that no one wants to work with (*the last child on the bench* in PE); and 'like with like' can fail to challenge and stimulate, can even stifle the introduction of new ideas, can become exclusive or elitist.
- Grouping by interest/enthusiasm is a fourth possibility. Although not really practical as a permanent arrangement it can be very powerful for short-term projects.

Children need to be in a position to work effectively as a group. The self-discipline required for greater concentration, perseverance and effective groupwork takes time to develop. Identifying things that they are good at is highly motivating. Encouraging children to articulate their feelings about themselves and their interests, likes and dislikes, is therefore a good starting point when trying to promote these skills. Readiness for groupwork can also be underpinned by providing common experiences for all the pupils involved, such as a class visit. Teachers of young children can look for indicators to help them assess the extent to which their children are improving and increasing their groupworking capabilities and readiness.

Groupwork indicators

Children
- can play cooperatively, work collaboratively, share and take turns;
- have developed positive relationships with others in the classroom, demonstrated by a willingness and an ability to initiate verbal and non-verbal interactions with adults and peers;
- are able and willing to participate in discussions;
- can identify the effects of their behaviour on others with help;
- are able to observe and adhere to rules and conventions such as accepting and respecting differences;
- are developing an ability to cope with change;
- are developing strategies for coping with frustration, for example, having another go or trying different approaches; and
- are displaying an increasing confidence to try things out independently.

The suggestions below may be helpful to trainee and newly qualified teachers when planning and managing groupwork sessions.

Managing young children's learning in groups

- Allow for variety and flexibility when grouping children; this is determined to some extent by the purposes or objectives of the activity and the fact that relationships change over time.
- Remember that younger children's need for security can be undermined by constantly chopping and changing groups.

- Capitalize on the similarities between pupils in order to make children feel more secure in groups.
- Capitalize on the differences between pupils in order to encourage creativity and excitement. Groups based on diversity can benefit from the challenges and tensions created by differences, but you must ensure that these challenges are tackled in a positive and supportive fashion.
- Ensure that everyone knows the purpose of the task.
- Offer the group guidance on procedures at the start, and remind them about class conventions and timescales.
- Do not play a numbers game. A group is not defined by the number 4 or 6. The larger the group, the easier it is for some young children to find themselves on the margins of an activity. The size of the group also interferes with procedure. It can take pupils all their time just to decide what they want to do and then there is no time left to do it.
- Think about roles in groups. Who is going to do what? Are there real roles for all?
- Consider your role in promoting effective groupwork:
  - When will adult interventions be needed?
  - Where will you be and what will you be doing while groupwork is taking place?
  - Have you made effective use of other adult support?
  - Provide opportunities for reflection about groupwork. For children to become better at groupwork they need to be given the chance to think about how they worked together. Praise and recognition reinforce desirable behaviour.
  - Do not attempt to chair multiple groups simultaneously yourself. Use a classroom map to predict potential clashes and avoid trying to be everywhere at once. Make sure that there are some sessions when groups engaged in stuctured play and practical and creative activities also receive higher levels of teacher attention.

Using a classroom map to plan for groupwork

- *Red*: high intervention. Needs you most/all of the time.
- *Orange/amber*: medium intervention. Needs you some of the time, for example, starting the group off and monitoring from a distance.
- *Green*: low intervention. Needs occasional visits and checks.

Classroom Map

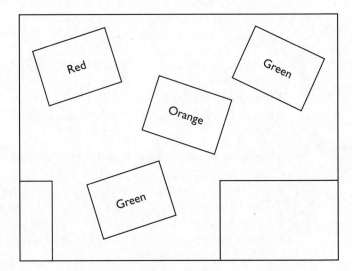

Organizing the Learning Environment

AUDIT

By the end of this section you should

- be familiar with ways of establishing safe environments for 3–8 pupils which support their learning and in which they feel secure and confident (B4j).

Educators of young children have to consider the ways in which learning takes place and is experienced by children as well as the content of the curriculum. How children are encouraged to learn is every bit as important as what they learn. Young children are like all learners – they are affected by their working environment and by the people who are working with them. An environment that is both stimulating and accessible provides support and encouragement for learning.

Resources and the Physical Environment

Some resources will be assigned to individual classes or teachers, some will be available to teams of staff (for example, the nursery team or the Y2 classes), others may be held centrally for use by the whole school. Within classrooms, many teachers operate a mixed economy with their equipment and resources. Some are teacher-controlled, others are open-access. The issue of access will often be shaped by concerns about health and safety, and classroom management. At the same time the physical environment should be welcoming and designed with younger children in mind. Safety gates and doors in nursery settings and scaled-down furniture in a reception/Y1 class are two examples.

Creating a safe learning environment: a checklist

Does the nursery/school have

- safety glass or plastic covering for low windows and doors
- well-lit stairways
- slow closing internal doors
- safety gates
- safe floor coverings
- fire-retardant curtains and soft furnishings
- guards on fires or radiators
- protected power sockets
- closely supervised use of heavy or sharp equipment
- fire exits clearly marked and accessible
- non-lockable toilets

- hygienic toilet facilities
- rubbish points that are inaccessible to children
- systems for recording and reporting accidents, especially head injuries
- safe car parking
- effective supervision of children before and after nursery/school
- effective supervision of children in the playground
- high standards of organization and management during off-site visits?

(Adapted from *Let's Get It Right*, Leeds City Council, Under Eights Service, 1996)

Using the outdoor space

An important resource and additional learning environment is the space outside the nursery/classroom. Many teachers of young children make extensive use of outdoor areas as a way of broadening their experience. These areas offer opportunities for play and physical development (see Chapter 1) and have the potential to support teaching and learning across the whole of the 3–8 curriculum. Well-designed outdoor learning environments will feature a range of flat and raised spaces, as well as a variety of soft and hard surfaces such as grass, sand and Tarmac. In addition, there will be a mixture of open and secluded areas to encourage group play and allow for individual activities. Benches and tables are important for teachers wishing to extend learning opportunities across the whole curriculum.

Ways to use the outdoor environment

Outdoor areas can foster play and promote physical development by including
- playground markings (snakes and ladders, footsteps);
- permanent apparatus and features (climbing frame, logs, stepping stones);
- small-scale play equipment (balls, quoits, bean bags, hoops, skipping ropes);
- large-scale play apparatus (see Chapter 1).

Outdoor areas can also promote pupils' development in the rest of the curriculum:
- tables and seating for reading and writing activities;
- listening to sounds, making music, painting and drawing can promote creative development and observational skills;
- sand and water troughs provide opportunities for exploratory and investigative work;
- bird tables, feeders and a garden/growing area offer children the chance to observe the natural world and learn about plants and animals;
- work on the weather (rain, puddles, wind, shadows) can add to children's knowledge of the world around them; and
- measuring and counting activities can offer new contexts within which to develop their mathematical skills and knowledge.

Managing the resources and the space in 3–8 settings

- In the case of shared resources and loans, advance action may well be needed in order to ensure access to them at the right moment; for example, booking library loans.

- When arranging and organizing classroom resources used on a daily basis consider ease of access and rules. Safety is a key factor when working with young children.
- Encourage pupils to make choices, to select equipment and materials, to take responsibility for keeping the classroom tidy, and to develop their own resource management skills.
- Do not put potentially hazardous tools and materials (such as hot glue guns) on open access. Ensure that children understand the importance of safety and restrict usage of some resources to adults only, or situations where strict supervision is available.
- Remember that teachers and other responsible adults are the most valuable resource available. High adult–child ratios help to make the most effective use of materials and equipment. They help to foster a sense of security, and are important in reinforcing learning in young children. Adults are also very important as role models for children.
- Plan and establish a mixture of clearly defined areas and general purpose spaces in the nursery/classroom. There should be sufficient and varied space for a range of activities, space that is clearly signposted or labelled.
- Label storage areas and containers with words *and* pictures. Encourage children to refer to the labels.
- Use furniture to mark out and define areas, including quiet areas, but bear in mind the need to be able to observe and monitor children.
- Some activities will be noisy and messy, others quiet and orderly. Different activities can be separated by time as well as by space.
- Try to keep messy activities near the sink.
- Include a wide range of interesting objects, materials and equipment to create a stimulating environment.
- Use bright, colourful, interesting and interactive displays.
- Make sure that any chemicals (such as cleaning fluids) and medicines are securely locked away.
- Make sure that the learning environment is properly cleaned. Teachers and children can help caretakers and cleaners by ensuring that the nursery/classroom is properly tidied up at the end of the day.
- Find out who the trained first aider on the staff team is.

Display

The use of display helps to create an attractive learning environment and plays a vital part in the process of motivating children, setting standards and communicating information to parents and other visitors about the children's experiences and work. A good display can start children talking, thinking, asking questions, and working, as well as offering a means of praising, recognizing and encouraging them. Putting children's work on display shows publicly the value that the teacher places on their efforts. Displays should be professionally presented; a sloppy display can make good work look poor and does not do justice to the efforts of the children. Finally, children's involvement in some of the decision-making about the what and how of displays can help to ensure that a display is used and referred to.

An unusual display

A class of Y2/3 children made a model of a Pteranadon out of bin liners (for wings) and large cardboard boxes. They painted it bright blue with red eyes the size of plates. One of the children had learned that no one could be sure what colour dinosaurs were but since it flew in the sky the pupils thought it should be blue. Their teacher decided to surprise the children by arriving especially early the next day and suspending the model from the ceiling. It took the children more than 30 minutes to notice the model hanging six feet above their heads.

Note: If young children can miss a prehistoric monster with a 10-metre wingspan, how much easier is it for them to miss a drawing or piece of writing?

Not all 3–8 teachers have artistic talents, nor is this necessary in order to produce a professional display. Trainee and newly qualified teachers may wish to make use of the checklist below when mounting displays in 3–8 settings.

Display checklist

- Whose work is displayed and why? If the aim is to motivate pupils, then it ought to be the children's work, not the teacher's, that is displayed.
- Include *effort* alongside *outcome* as criteria for judging which pieces of work are put on show. If effort is not used as a criterion for selection, then some children may be consistently overlooked while others may receive disproportionate recognition.
- Make sure that displays reflect the variety and breadth of the 3–8 curriculum, showing practical activities as well as written work, celebrating personal and social development as well as academic achievement, and showing the development of skills as well as the acquisition of knowledge.
- Utilize a range of techniques which include two-dimensional as well as three-dimensional ones, and hands-on interactive displays as well as static ones.
- Use your displays in your teaching.
- Change displays on a regular basis.
- Ensure that displays are professionally presented.
  - Mounts cut straight and even, with square corners.
  - Margins equal. If they are unequal, this should be deliberate.
  - Provide labels with correct spellings and the children's names.
  - Handwriting on the display should conform to the nursery's/school's guidelines?
  - Remember that the spaces between work are as important as those occupied by the work. Avoid overcrowding.
  - Check the height and level.
  - Does the display conform to school/nursery conventions (e.g. single/double mounted, limited colour schemes)?
  - An overall impression of neatness and tidiness, with evidence of pride taken.

Ethos and Equality of Opportunity

A key concern for teachers when thinking about organizing a high-quality learning environment is the ethos of the setting, including equality of opportunity. The ethos in nursery and primary settings is informed by the Education Reform Act 1988. Under the Act, all children have a right to expect that their teachers will provide them with every opportunity to achieve their full potential irrespective of their gender, race, ability or social class. They are entitled to an education that will enable them to participate fully in society, an education that prepares them for the opportunities, responsibilities, choices and experiences of adult life (NCC, 1990).

Adult conduct is central to the task of establishing a learning environment in which the ethos is supportive of all the pupils. When working to identify and address the individual needs of children, teachers must be careful not to fall into the trap of making stereotypical assumptions about the children's intellectual, emotional, social and physical attributes (Adams, 1994). Staff expectations can have a powerful influence on children's achievement and self-esteem.

Equality of opportunity is a complex and sometimes difficult issue facing teachers. In their desire not to be unfair to children, some teachers adopt the position of trying to 'treat everyone the same'. This is sometimes the result of an understandable wish to avoid making mistakes that give offence and possibly cause conflict. However, treating all children in the same way does not ensure equality of opportunity, but has quite the reverse effect. Such a policy ignores and fails to tackle the individual needs and differences of children. It is also a mistake to think that young children themselves are ignorant of the differences between them. They can be very conscious of them and may have their attention drawn to these differences outside of school and nursery. To pretend that such differences do not exist, and to fail to celebrate diversity and to encourage respect for these differences, is to imply that there is something wrong about them. The social and cultural diversity that exists in Britain today needs to be viewed as an asset and not as a problem to be evaded. The education of 3–8 pupils should include the promotion of positive attitudes towards diversity. Those teaching young children play a key role in fostering such positive attitudes when children are most receptive to new ideas.

Creating an inclusive learning environment

- Group classes to ensure a balance in terms of gender, race, ability and class.
- Make concerts and assemblies inclusive of all groups in the nursery/school, including good work assemblies.
- Include non-teaching staff (for example, playtime and lunchtime supervisors) in discussions about the nursery/school equal opportunities policy and help to develop appropriate strategies to translate the principles into practice.
- Provide resources that actively and positively promote the diversity of culture, class and gender roles in society.

- Use attractive and professionally presented displays that incorporate objects, ideas, and visual and written material from a range of cultures and geographical locations.
- Ensure that the principle of equality of opportunity permeates planning and teaching and that the curriculum is enriched and enhanced by positive reference to diversity.
- Deal promptly and efficiently with biased or discriminatory attitudes and actions. Discriminatory behaviour, including bullying, on the basis of differences in terms of gender, race or class is unacceptable. Nurseries and schools should operate a policy of 'zero tolerance' and staff should ensure that when such incidents occur pupils are encouraged to confront their assumptions, actions and the consequences of those actions.
- Work to develop a shared understanding of the nursery/school policy and practices amongst parents, governors and other staff.
- Help children to identify the similarities, as well as the differences, that exist between them and their classmates. Help them to understand the differences and to behave in a considerate manner.

Effective Teaching Methods

By the end of this section you should

- know about a range of teaching methods which will help to sustain the momentum of pupils' work and keep pupils engaged (B4ki-xiv);
- know about the place of self-evaluation in improving effectiveness in the nursery/classroom (B4n).

As a trainee teacher or newly qualified teacher, it is important to learn about and acquire a range of effective teaching strategies as soon as possible. Without the ability to do this, the learning opportunities planned for the children may never be realized. This section concentrates on some of the key skills 3–8 teachers need to acquire in order to be effective in the nursery/classroom. It will touch upon one aspect which is often at the forefront of trainees' and NQTs' minds – discipline and control. This aspect of teaching and class management is important and we return to it in Chapter 4. However, although good discipline is a necessary prerequisite for successful teaching, it is not a sufficient condition on its own and it must be underpinned by positive professional teaching methods.

Awareness and Mobility

Expect the unexpected

A newly qualified teacher had just finished a very well-organized and structured PE lesson with a Y1/Y2 class. The children were getting changed at one end of the hall and the teacher moved away from them for a short time to return some balls to a box. On the teacher's return, Suzanne approached her to say that she could not find her leotard. Everyone helped to look for it, corners were explored, kit bags were emptied, apparatus boxes were opened. Every possible place where a leotard might have been mislaid was investigated. There appeared to be no sign of it. Meanwhile the class was becoming unsettled and disruptive. The next class was queuing to come into the hall, and their well-established teacher was looking disapprovingly through the glass. A horrible suspicion began to dawn on the NQT. 'Suzanne, just lift your T-shirt up one moment will you please?' She did, and the mystery was solved: she was still wearing the leotard!

Teachers of young children need to maintain a high degree of vigilance at all times. This awareness, sometimes referred to as *withitness*, is a crucial skill for anyone attempting to ensure high quality teaching and effective class management with 3–8 pupils. It takes time to develop a fully-fledged appreciation of young children; however, it is possible to acquire and master the skills associated with awareness by making a conscious effort in the early stages of training and teaching. Retaining a degree of mobility in the classroom greatly increases a teacher's awareness; the mere presence or proximity of an adult has a calming and controlling effect. Simply being there can do much to help young children stay on task. At the same time, moving around can also help to avoid long queues of children requesting the teacher's attention. Finally, awareness and mobility are important prerequisite skills for identifying and consolidating children's learning.

Maintaining your awareness

- Make a point of scanning the immediate teaching area at intervals.
- Remember to check to the sides and rear.
- Demonstrate a degree of prescience by trying to anticipate events.
- Make a conscious effort to listen to the noise in the classroom; there is a qualitative difference between a busy hum and the sound of children who are off-task.

Communication

Preparing the ground

Mrs Clark asked all her Y1s to stop what they were doing and look at her. After a minute or so, during which time she asked one or two individuals by name to look her way, she then informed the children that in five minutes they would have to start clearing away ready to go to assembly. She asked the children to start to finish off the piece of work that they were doing, and checked with one or two 'key' individuals that they had understood what they had to do. When Mrs Clark stopped the children again five minutes later and asked them to start clearing up, the transition went very smoothly – the children were prepared for the task.

The ability to communicate effectively and appropriately with young children is another essential teaching skill.

Teachers of young children use their communication skills in the nursery/classroom to

- generate interest and curiosity;
- review and consolidate previous learning;
- share the programme and purposes of a session/lesson;
- maintain control; and
- offer encouragement and support.

Clear and concise instructions play a valuable part in effective classroom organization and management, while exposition (discussing, explaining and outlining things verbally), is one way in which a teacher can inspire and motivate children (Waterhouse, 1983). That said, by their very nature, discussions of this sort are likely to involve a few departures. Teachers need to be ready to deal sensitively but efficiently with unexpected contributions, taking on board children's comments while avoiding being sidetracked.

Gentle steering of a discussion

A class of Y1 children were listening and responding to questions about a story that their teacher was reading. The teacher asked the children what they thought was about to happen. Ellen put up her hand and the teacher said, 'Yes Ellen. What do you think will happen?' Ellen responded 'I went to my Gran's on Saturday'. The teacher replied, 'Did you? That's very interesting, do you think you could tell us a bit more about it when we've finished our story? Thank you. Now then, can anyone tell us what they think is going to happen next?'

Improving verbal communication with children

- Exposition, including any questioning and discussion, ought to be thought about beforehand. A list of key questions and useful vocabulary can be helpful.
- Use a wide range of questioning techniques including open-ended and closed, procedural (e.g. What are they trying to do?), and organizational (e.g. How are they going to do something?).
- Use question and answer times to make judgements about children's understanding and learning needs, and to pick up on any ideas or misconceptions.
- When discussing things with young children or asking questions, be prepared to show a little patience while they marshal their thoughts.
- Use praise and recognition to foster participation.
- Be inclusive. Avoid addressing the front and centre of the group or class while ignoring pupils at the back and sides.
- Promote respect for others. Follow rules, such as *hands up*.
- Make sure that instructions are clear and concise and that you have the children's attention before giving them.

- Do not string multiple instructions together. Young children may not be able to remember them all.
- Check that your instructions have been understood.

Monitoring the Learning Process

While planning and preparation are important prerequisites for effective 3–8 education, teachers still have to make their plans work. They have to control the learning process, ensuring that the timing and pacing of activities is appropriate, that transitions between tasks are managed smoothly and that children's progress is monitored and consolidated in an ongoing fashion.

Monitoring and consolidating learning

- Have a clear focus for the activity or lesson and share this with the children.
- Think about checking and monitoring that needs to take place during a lesson/session. Retaining a degree of mobility will help you to do at least some of this checking and monitoring as you go along. Ongoing monitoring has two advantages. First, it enables you to consolidate learning and assist children with problems and difficulties at point of need and reduces your work at break time and at the end of the day. Second, it shows children that you are interested in and value their work; this can be a powerful source of motivation.
- Have a clearly identified location, where work is to be placed, such as a finished work box. This makes it easier to locate the material for checking or marking and stops a lot of time-consuming queries from children.
- Base your standards and expectations on your knowledge of the children's abilities and include attention to the process of learning as well as to the outcomes of that process. The ever-increasing accountability of teachers places pressure on them to prioritize the finished product, but the commitment shown by the children, their willingness to concentrate and persevere, and their ability to cooperate and work constructively and positively with their peers ought to be equally important.
- If engaged on a teaching practice with unfamiliar pupils or working with your first class, look back at previous work from time-to-time. It can be a useful way of identifying pupils whose work seems to be deteriorating rather than progressing.
- When errors or misconceptions arise, deal with them in a sensitive and humane fashion.

Promoting Good Behaviour

Promoting pride in good behaviour

In our class we share things and look after things.
In our class we look after one another.
In our class we are kind to one another.
In our class we put things back where they came from.
In our class we don't shout.
In our class we don't run.

Establishing and maintaining simple conventions and routines within the nursery/classroom underpins a teacher's efforts to achieve good class management. Not only are ground rules important from the point of view of health and safety, but of equal validity, young children feel much more secure in an environment where certain boundaries are clearly marked out (Dean, 1993). Establishing such conventions can require a major effort at the beginning of a year or term. However, such an investment will more than repay the teacher as the year progresses.

Establishing conventions

- Try to establish conventions that are appropriate for the age and maturity of the children.
- Use praise and recognition to positively reinforce desired behaviour.
- Give clear recognition to displays of honesty, fairness and respect.
- Help children to understand 'right' and 'wrong' behaviours.
- Be consistent about conventions through firm, though gentle, insistence.
- Where minor infractions occur handle the situation in a calm, firm and fair manner.
- Keep conventions simple and few in number so that they are manageable and understandable.
- Discuss conventions with children in terms of personal responsibility, consequences and feelings so that they can appreciate their importance.
- Remember that obedience is a means to an end, not an end in itself. Although conventions underpin good behaviour in the nursery/classroom, so too does experience of freedom and making choices. It is through being able to exercise their decision-making skills that children can begin to grow up into responsible, independent and self-disciplined adults. Such abilities cannot be acquired simply through being told, they need to be fostered by first-hand experience.

Matching conventions to situations

Instances where conventions might apply:
- lunchtime
- putting things away
- not taking things that do not belong to you
- not running across roads, hitting, or biting
- movement as a class (to PE, assembly, or out to play)
- movement by individuals within the class, (Does it have a purpose? Does it limit the freedom of others?)
- noise levels (not shouting out but raising hands, listening while others speak, using normal voices when speaking individually to one another)
- handling equipment and materials sensibly (lifting, not dragging, chairs).

Instances where free choice and decision making might be promoted:

- choosing games and toys
- choosing which friends to work with
- choosing which activity to go to
- developing role-play scenarios
- selecting equipment.

Teacher Expectations

The teacher is hugely influential in children's learning and development. Trainee and newly qualified teachers need only to think back to their own school days to appreciate the important role that their expectations can play in a child's achievement. The more persistent low expectations are, the greater their impact on a child's self-esteem and the more deep rooted their low- or under-achievement is likely to become. Having appropriate and demanding expectations of children involves consideration of both their behaviour and their work.

Expectations relating to behaviour

These expectations are closely linked to the ground rules or conventions referred to in the previous section, and relate to equality of opportunity and conduct. Children can be included in deciding on what form they will have as a way of encouraging them to take ownership of, and responsibility for, this classroom ethos (Roberts, 1983). Like learning purposes, such expectations need to be communicated to the children and reinforced at every opportunity.

Expectations of general behaviour

Teachers expect children to
- walk, not run, around the classroom;
- seek permission before leaving the room or area;
- listen to others;
- converse in normal voices without shouting;
- take care when handling tools and materials;
- show care and consideration for their peers irrespective of race, gender, ability or class; and
- show care for the learning environment.

Expectations relating to work

These expectations are based on an appreciation of the needs and capabilities of the pupils. In part this means finding out about them as learners, a task that may be informed by school records, discussions with colleagues, contact with parents and the children themselves. Engaging in conversation with children and listening to them, as well as monitoring and observing their work, will assist you in seeking out materials and experiences likely to appeal to pupils and offer opportunities for them to follow up on some of their interests. Thinking about Gardner's intelligences (see p. 68) can help you to interpret children's comments, actions and achievements.

Which children
• are highly inquisitive and curious?;
• are self-confident, adventurous, and enjoy decision-making?;
• are in need of more support and encouragement to take risks and respond positively to new things and experiences?;
• thrive on practical problems?;
• prefer intellectual problems?;
• are quiet, steady, composed?;
• are gregarious?;
• enjoy the written word?;
• prefer the spoken word?;
• find visual information most instructive?

Expectations and achievement

Teachers *expect* children to
• try their hardest;
• take pride in their work;
• concentrate;
• listen; and
• participate.

Being a Reflective Practitioner

Trainee and newly qualified teachers who engage in self-evaluation (critically reflecting on their practice and how to improve it) are likely to master a wider range of effective teaching methods more quickly than those who do not (Bengtsson, 1995). Such evaluation can be used to improve performance over both the long and short term. Evaluation is not simply a summative task to complete at the end of a lesson on teaching practice. Good teachers evaluate their practice formatively and constantly. It is this informal evaluation that generates a decision to rephrase something differently in order to communicate an idea more effectively, or encourages a teacher to pick up the pace of a lesson in response to the early signs of fidgeting.

Evaluating teaching and learning

• When noting down evaluative remarks as evidence for tutors and school mentors, bullet points can provide a manageable and efficient approach.

- Start with what went well. Why did it go well? How do you know? What is your evidence?
- Was there an aspect of the lesson/session that did not go well? Why was this? How do you know? What is your evidence?
- To what extent were your teaching objectives (knowledge, skills, attitudes, new vocabulary) achieved? How do you know? What is your evidence?
- Was the lesson content too hard/too easy/just right? For whom? How do you know? What is your evidence?
- How effective was your organization and management (timing, pace, resources, transitions)? How do you know? What is your evidence?
- To what extent were good order and a positive learning atmosphere maintained? How do you know? What is your evidence?
- What would you do differently in the future? Why?
- What should the children do next?

Managing Other Adults and Working as Part of a Team

AUDIT

By the end of this section you should

- be aware of strategies for improving your expertise in working with other adults including parents and carers (A3b);
- know about some of the other professionals involved in the care and education of young children (A3c);
- be familiar with a range of strategies for managing the work of other adults in the nursery/classroom (B5h).

Having other adults in the nursery/classroom, in addition to the teacher, can significantly enhance children's learning. The involvement of other adults in 3–8 settings means that teachers need to be effective both as leaders and as members of a team.

The Teacher as Team Worker and Leader

In some instances, the additional adult support available to 3–8 teachers is on a voluntary basis; in others, the support is professional in nature and may involve a wide variety of staff, both internal and external. In all cases, teachers should value adult support and treat those involved with respect. While not necessarily trained as teachers themselves, other adults can bring skill and experience to the learning environment. Teachers need to be able to make the most of this expertise.

It is the teacher's job to take responsibility for managing this valuable human resource. At one level this involves decisions about which activities and pupils adult support staff should be responsible for, and discussing with them the purposes and processes of lessons or activities. However, teachers also need to think about the wider curriculum which includes the ethos and philosophy of the nursery/classroom. Non-teaching adult support can be effective in helping to inculcate in young children values and expectations such as fairness, respect and honesty. The ability to manage, lead and take responsibility for a team, some of whose members might only be occasional visitors, is a demanding task. It can be particularly challenging for trainees and newly qualified teachers whose experience is still limited in relation to many of the other adults they are being asked to manage. It is a real test of teachers' interpersonal skills as well as their professional expertise to do this successfully.

Clearly, team working abilities and good communication skills are essential for a coherent approach. In the case of planning, for example, a team approach enables staff to

- produce a more comprehensive set of learning opportunities;
- improve their individual capabilities by learning from one another;
- utilize particular strengths;
- promote continuity and progression; and
- ensure a unified and coherent philosophy and ethos.

In nurseries especially, the teamwork required is particularly noticeable, including as it does both the core nursery team (nursery teachers, nursery nurses and child-care assistants) and the wider team (language support staff, special needs staff and parents). Some of the skills and qualities needed by teachers when leading or working in a team are listed below.

Leadership and team working skills and qualities

- assertiveness
- determination
- consideration towards the feelings of others
- energy
- creativity
- flexibility
- ability to focus clearly on a task
- well organized approach
- excellent communication skills
- ability to delegate
- knowledgeable about young children and the curriculum
- good negotiating skills
- being thoughtful and reflective
- good problem-solving abilities
- ability to motivate and support others

This list makes clear the demanding nature of team work. Although there is no foolproof method for responding to this challenge, there are certain principles that teachers ought to keep in mind when considering the best ways to organize and manage the work of other adults in the nursery/classroom.

Improving your expertise in working with other adults

- **Thinking ahead**. Planning and preparation enhance your chances of success.
- **Participation**. The whole team should be involved (in appropriate ways) in planning, organizing and managing the learning environment.
- **Communication**. If you fail to discuss your intentions and ideas with non-teaching colleagues or fail to listen to their ideas and observations, there is a danger of inconsistency in approach and outcomes.
- **Leading by example**. This is something that you are already experienced in through your interactions with children. If you wish to foster a positive, supportive and calm manner in other adults it helps to exhibit those qualities and characteristics yourself.
- **Reviewing**. Being a reflective practitioner and reviewing the outcomes of using non-teaching support are essential if your skills and capabilities in this area are to improve.

Who are the other Adults?

The following paragraphs deal briefly with some of the other adults who may be involved in the 3–8 settings.

Nursery nurses

Nursery nurses are trained in child development and health care, including early language development, numeracy, and personal and social development. They are also knowledgeable about the organization and management of early learning environments. They are an important part of the teaching team in a nursery/reception classroom. In terms of their interactions with the children, the responsibilities are very similar to those of teachers – the preparation of materials, setting out equipment, and facilitating children's learning. It can sometimes be difficult at first glance in many nurseries to distinguish between the teachers and the nursery nurses. The teacher, however, is ultimately responsible for planning and organizing both the curriculum and the day-to-day running of the nursery/classroom, albeit in consultation and collaboration with the nursery nurse(s).

Child-care assistants (CCAs) and non-teaching assistants (NTAs)

Very often, schools must share ancillary support staff between classes. Ancillary staff can take on some of the daily routines such as mounting pictures, thus freeing more teacher time for planning and teaching. Equally important however, is their ability to work alongside the teacher to extend and enhance the quality of educational provision for the children by targeting children who need extra support, giving valuable one-to-one attention to pupils, and encouraging children to talk, discuss and extend their speaking and listening skills (reading stories and listening to readers).

Parent volunteers

Teachers of 3–8 children endeavour to make the transition from home to school a positive one for children. This requires close cooperation with parents and it is in everyone's interests to make parents feel a part of the teaching team. Unlike other adults who may work alongside the teacher in the nursery or classroom, parents have a unique relationship with at least one of the children present. Some parents may not have had happy school experiences themselves, and shyness or brusqueness might be signs of nervousness. As a result, it may be necessary to relieve parental anxiety by encouraging questions and making a conscious effort to be welcoming and approachable.

Working with parents

- Be prepared to discuss current educational ideas and practices with parents. Things may well have changed dramatically since their own school days.
- Remember that you might feel you are approachable, but others may not share that view. Be open with parents, show them that you can be discreet and will refrain from gossiping. Parents need to be sure that they can talk to you in confidence.
- Show parents that you listen to their comments and take their concerns seriously by taking action where necessary.

* For further information on working with parents see Chapter 4.

Other non-teaching colleagues (school secretaries, lunchtime supervisors, caretakers)

Effective liaison between teaching staff and non-teaching colleagues not directly involved in classroom activities is frequently undervalued. Both groups may need to talk about problems that particular children have and need to discuss what might constitute appropriate action in particular circumstances. New children can be supported in adapting to a new school/nursery environment by special and friendly attention during lunchtimes. Some pupils have allergies and other medical conditions which the teacher knows about but which also need to be communicated to other responsible adults.

Visiting and temporary members of the team

Nurseries and schools may at various times be visited be a wide variety of adults in both professional and volunteer capacities, all of whom may need to be included in a team approach, albeit on a temporary basis.

These visitors include:

- nurses;
- speech therapists;
- health visitors;
- Educational Welfare Officers (EWOs);
- educational psychologists;
- special needs staff;
- language support staff;
- students; and
- one-off visitors (community police officers, local theatre groups).

Health visitors and nurses conduct medical examinations of children, for example when they start nursery or school. They also carry out screening for possible problems such as hearing loss or visual impairment at regular intervals. Although many children with these difficulties are identified prior to starting school, others are not, and teachers have an important part to play in helping health professionals identify and assist pupils with difficulties.

Educational Welfare Officers (EWOs) are mainly concerned with the enforcement of compulsory school attendance. However, they can also be involved in wider aspects of child welfare such as neglect or illegal employment. In addition, EWOs may be involved in supplying adequate clothing, meals and transport for pupils from poor homes. EWOs are a useful link between teachers and the local social services.

Many schools and nurseries will draw on the expertise of individuals beyond the world of education in an effort to make the curriculum more relevant and exciting. Some of these experts may be parents or relatives. A good visitor can do much to motivate and enthuse children. Teachers must however bear in mind that while the visitors may have considerable expertise in their particular field, it is the teacher who is the child specialist. There is an onus upon the teacher to liaise with outside experts beforehand to ensure that the content will be appropriate for the children and that it will be presented in a suitable manner.

Poor liaison, poor teaching

An education officer from one of the public utilities was asked to come and talk to a class of Y1/2s about his industry as part of a project that the children had been doing. When the education officer arrived he set up his slide projector and overhead projector. He then delivered the same 45-minute talk that he used with secondary school leavers to a class of stunned infants and their equally stunned teacher. Thereafter, this particular NQT made a point of liaising properly, and in advance, with such visitors.

Strategies for making the best use of non-teaching support in the classroom

- Gather information on the role of non-teaching supporters and their expectations of you.
- Find out the procedures for briefing non-teaching colleagues.
- Explain what children should be learning and not just what they should do.
- Ensure that children understand the adult's role and behave properly.
- Prepare lessons which include plans for the work of other adults and review these in lesson evaluations.
- Remember that communication is vital.
- Develop shared policies on discipline, organization and assessment.
- Promote a team-working approach.
- Value the different perspectives that other adults bring.
- Avoid stereotypical or negative assumptions about non-teaching colleagues.
- Utlize the skills and talents of support staff.
- Give specific tasks to parents and volunteers in order to make them feel useful.
- Maintain confidentiality at all times.

(Suschitsky and Garner, 1995)

98

TEACHING 3–8

FURTHER SOURCES OF INFORMATION

Planning the 3–8 Curriculum

Alexander, R., Rose, J. and Woodhead, C. (1992) *Curriculum Organisation and Classroom Practice in Primary Schools: A Discussion Paper*. London: DES.

Qualifications and Curriculum Authority (1999) *The review of the desirable outcomes for children's learning on entering compulsory education*. London: QCA.

Rodger, R. (1999) *Planning an Appropriate Curriculum for the Under Fives*. London: David Fulton Publishers.

SCAA (1995) *Planning the Curriculum at Key Stages 1 and 2*. London: SCAA.

Individual Pupil Needs and Abilities

Cotton, J. (1995) *The Theory of Learners: An Introduction*. London: Kogan Page.

Cotton, J. (1995) *The Theory of Learning: An Introduction*. London: Kogan Page.

Morrison, K. and Ridley, K. (1988) *Curriculum Planning and the Primary School*. London: Chapman.

Naylor, S. and Keogh, B. (1995) 'Making differentiation manageable', *School Science Review*, **77** December, pp. 106–10.

Stradling, B. and Saunders, L. (1993) 'Differentiation in practice: responding to the needs of all pupils', *Educational Research*, **35** (2) Summer, pp. 127–37.

Children with Special Educational Needs (SEN)

Dearing, R. (1993) *The National Curriculum and its Assessment*. London: SCAA.

Hart, S. (1996) *Beyond Special Needs*. London: Chapman.

Roffey, S. (1999) *Special Needs in the Early Years: Collaboration, Communication and Coordination*. London: David Fulton Publishers.

Sharman, C., Cross, W. and Vennis, D. (1999) *Observing Children: A Practical Guide* (2nd edn). London: Cassell.

Organizing the Children and Class Management

Beard, J. and Lloyd, C. (1995) *Managing Classroom Collaboration*. London: Cassell.

Smith, C. J. and Laslett, R. (1993) *Effective Classroom Management: A Teacher's Guide, 2nd edn*. London: Routledge.

Wragg, E. C. (1993) *Class Management*. London: Routledge.

Organizing the Learning Environment

Bitton, H. (1998) *Outdoor Play in the Early Years: Management and Innovation*. London: David Fulton Publishers.

Cole, M. and Hill, D. (eds) (1997) *Promoting Equality in Primary Schools*. London: Cassell.

Dean, J. (1993) *Organising Learning in the Primary School, 3rd Edition*. London: Croom Helm.

Equal Opportunities Commission (1982) *Do you Provide Equal Educational Opportunities?* Manchester: EOC.

Equal Opportunities Commission (1984) *An Equal Start: Guidelines for those working with the under-fives*. Manchester: EOC.

Effective Teaching Methods

Merrett, F. and Wheldall, K. (1990) *Positive Teaching in the Primary School*. London: Chapman.

Pollard, A. (1997) *Reflective Teaching in the Primary School, 3rd edn*. London: Cassell.

Waterhouse, P. (1983) *Managing the Learning Process*. New York: McGraw-Hill.

Managing Other Adults and Working as Part of a Team

Day, C. W., Hall, C. and Whitaker, P. (1998) *Developing Leadership in Primary Schools*. London: Chapman.

Edgington, M. (1998) *The Nursery Teacher in Action: Teaching 3-, 4- and 5-year olds, 2nd edn*. London: Chapman Publishing.

Moyles, J. (ed.) (1995) *Beginning Teaching: Beginning Learning in Primary Education*. Buckingham: Open University Press.

Roffey, S. (1999) *Special Needs in the Early Years: Collaboration Communication and Coordination*. London: David Fulton Publishers.

3

Monitoring, Assessment, Recording, Reporting and Accountability

SUMMARY

Assessment of children's learning is not a new role for 3–8 teachers, nor is record keeping and reporting. Teachers have always made judgements about their pupils and have used those judgements in structuring their future teaching. However, the introduction of the National Curriculum and Desirable Outcomes/Early Learning Goals and the increasing pressures associated with monitoring and public accountability have greatly increased the amount of time and rigour being applied to this aspect of the teacher's tasks.

The results of assessment are an integral and indispensable part of the teaching and learning process. All teachers need to be proficient at monitoring and assessing children's learning, as well as recording and reporting their progress. Although nursery and many reception teachers are not subject to the requirements of the National Curriculum, monitoring, assessment, recording, reporting and accountability are equally important aspects of effective teaching and learning.

By the end of this chapter you should

- know about the use of assessment information on pupils' attainment in teaching and in planning future lessons and sequences of lessons (B4c, Cc);
- know about alternative forms and methods of assessment (Ca, Ci);
- know about methods of recording children's progress and achievements (Cb, Cc); and
- know about reporting to parents on pupils' progress including reports on SATs and baseline assessments (Cd,h,i).

Monitoring and Assessing 3–8 Pupils

By the end of this section you should

- know about alternative forms and methods of assessing young children (Ca);
- know about using assessment to improve teaching (Cc);
- know about using different kinds of assessment for different purposes (Ci).

Why Assess?

Assessing young children involves more than simply looking at the work they produce. Teachers need to employ their observation and questioning skills in order to ascertain what children know, what they can do and where they need to go next. All this takes time, a resource that is in short supply in nurseries and classrooms. If teachers wish to justify this time, they need first to be clear about why assessment matters.

Assessment benefits all those involved in the education of young children, including the teachers and other professionals, the children themselves, and their parents. The primary purposes of assessment are: firstly to improve the quality of teaching and learning; and secondly to enable schools and nurseries to report on children's progress and provide summative information on their achievements.

- For *teachers*, assessment provides a better understanding of children's learning. It offers a way to ensure progression and greater continuity for pupils as the results of assessment provide reliable information upon which to plan the next step of a teaching programme. It is a process which provides information on individual pupil experience and achievement across the curriculum, providing a way of investigating and identifying progress in terms of what a child knows, understands and can do. The results of assessment also provide teachers with a more valid base for evaluating the curriculum, helping them to monitor and raise standards (DfEE, 1990).
- Assessment is helpful to *children*. It enhances their motivation and confidence through the promotion of accurate and constructive feedback from the teacher in the form of short-term learning targets and the identification of future learning needs.
- Assessment is helpful for *parents and others*, including future teachers and the wider community, who wish to evaluate the effectiveness of a nursery/school through teachers' reports (both verbal and written), SATs results. Assessment can also provide information on pupil attainment to date that can be used to make the transition within and between schools more streamlined.

Assessing the youngest children

As with older children, nursery and reception teachers assess pupils in order to

- inform future learning experiences by celebrating and building on successes and diagnosing and responding to difficulties;
- inform parents and future teachers about children's achievements to date;
- help children to set targets for future learning; and
- evaluate their own practice and provision.

Those working with nursery and reception pupils may have a clear focus for assessment and structure their interventions and the activities to give children opportunities to demonstrate achievement. On other occasions useful information may be obtained from unplanned observations of pupils. Parents too can play a particularly important role in effective assessment of 3–5 year olds. The logical extension of the idea that parents are important partners in their children's education is that they have a part to play in early assessment. Initial assessments of nursery children, for example, can be greatly enhanced by parental input.

An early assessment sheet completed jointly by parents and nursery teacher

Name:

Date of birth:

Admission date:

Asks questions e.g. Why? Who? When? Where? What? ☐

Independence/decision-making skills ☐

Expresses needs and wants, using speech and gestures ☐

Comments and directs e.g. 'Come on', 'I like' ☐

Uses language in play ☐

Joins in conversations/interchanges with three or more turns ☐

Listens to and enjoys books, songs and poems ☐

Book skills ☐

Understands that print carries meaning ☐

Reads own 'writing' ☐

Can recognize own name ☐

Knows letter sounds ☐

Scribbling ☐   Writing ☐
Letter shapes ☐   Key words ☐

Colour identification

red ☐   blue ☐   yellow ☐
green ☐   orange ☐   purple ☐
black ☐   brown ☐   pink ☐
white ☐

Shape identification

square ☐   circle ☐   triangle ☐
rectangle ☐   oval ☐   star ☐

Matching

by colour ☐   by shape ☐
by type ☐   by more than one attribute ☐

Sorting

by colour ☐   by shape ☐
by type ☐   by more than one attribute ☐

Counting   1–5 ☐   5–10 ☐
more than 10 ☐

Number symbol/ quantity ☐

Conservation of number ☐

Ordering ☐

Follows pattern and sequence ☐

Time ☐

Can order

by size ☐   big/little ☐
short/tall ☐   heavy/light ☐
full/empty ☐

Reports previous experiences ☐

Identifies and describes similarities and differences ☐

Reasoning skills ☐

Ability to predict ☐

Play

Solitary ☐   Parallel ☐   Cooperative ☐
Exploratory ☐   Self-pretend ☐
Sequence pretend ☐

Fine motor skills e.g. threading, small construction, pencil, brush, glue spreader, scissors ☐

Gross motor skills

coordination ☐   balancing ☐
climbing ☐   riding ☐
catching ☐   kicking ☐
throwing ☐

103

MONITORING, ASSESSMENT, RECORDING, REPORTING AND ACCOUNTABILITY

- In reception classes, where staffing levels are often lower than those in nursery, good organization and planning are essential if a parental contribution is to be obtained in a time-scale of use to you.
- Initial assessments involving parents in the nursery/classroom may necessitate provision for the care of younger siblings while discussions take place.
- Parents need to be reassured that the information they are supplying is for positive reasons and will not be used to discriminate against their child.
- Parents need to know that in instances where special educational needs are identified some of the information they give may also be passed on to other professionals involved in the education and welfare of young children.

Forms of Assessment

Assessment takes various forms and it is important to realize that the boundaries between these different forms are not always clearly delineated. It can be difficult, for example, to determine whether assessment is summative or formative in nature; considerable overlap is possible.

Criterion-referenced and norm-referenced assessment

Assessment that is criterion-referenced seeks to assess pupils' achievement against a set of standards or competences, utilizing increasingly more demanding descriptions to judge and report on attainment. Such criteria can be helpful for teachers in sharing the purpose of the activity with the children. Unfortunately, producing criteria or descriptions that are universally understood and unambiguous is not as easy as it might sound. The National Curriculum level descriptions are an example of criterion-referenced assessment; the Standards for the Award of Qualified Teacher Status are another.

Norm-referenced assessment involves making comparisons between the achievements of a child and those of their peers. The norms in question are intended to describe an average or typical performance; they are not intended as standards or desirable levels of attainment.

Formal and informal assessment

Informal assessment is an activity in which teachers are constantly involved, for example using a smile, a frown, spoken comments on the amount of effort being made, or written comments on pieces of work. This type of assessment provides a very wide-ranging evidence base, considered over an extended period of time. It makes an invaluable contribution to formative assessment and acts as the basis for a considerable amount of good quality and immediate feedback to pupils.

Informal assessment is such a normal part of classroom life that it can be over-looked and is sometimes undervalued.

Informal assessment may occur

- as a result of routine discussions and observations. Children's answers to teachers' questions are evaluated by those teachers, who then make judgements about the children's level of understanding. Similarly, children's comments and behaviour may reveal unplanned for, and unanticipated, evidence causing a teacher to assess the situation and take action:

Routine observation

John and Ruth had been paired to work on a design and technology activity. It became clear to the teacher from their expressions that John was feeling self-conscious about working with a girl and that Ruth was well aware of his attitude. Although the learning objectives were centred around the subject, the teacher had an ongoing commitment to encourage children to work constructively together. She responded immediately to her informal assessment of the situation by intervening quickly to offer encouragement and support to both children and to help them to organize themselves to tackle the activity in such a way that both children had real roles in the task.

- through examining work produced. Informal assessment can also occur as a result of looking at the concrete outcomes of activities:

Examining work produced

Miss Lee was moving around her class of Y1/2s who were engaged in number work activities as part of their regular numeracy hour. She noticed that two or three children were making the same mistake. She intervened to help the children to tackle the problem individually and made a note to pursue the matter with this group in a subsequent lesson.

Formal assessment takes place when teachers have planned for it, times have been identified and the results will be formally recorded:

Formal assessment

Mrs Jones had been conducting formal assessments of her children's scientific skills, knowledge and understanding during the week. The focus was on forces and in particular, floating and sinking. She had arranged for non-teaching support and/or parents to be in the classroom while she assessed the children in groups. The children were testing objects in the water tank and discussing their observations and ideas with Mrs Jones who was noting down any evidence of attainment against a checklist. She asked the children to predict which objects would float and which ones would sink. Wayne suggested that the apple would float. Mrs Jones asked him to explain why he thought this was the case. 'Because it was floating this morning miss.'

Summative assessment

Some assessments will be summative in nature and result in statements about what a child has achieved at a particular point in time, for example, on transition from the nursery to the reception class, or at the end of Key Stage 1. A summative assessment constitutes a record of the overall achievement of a pupil in a systematic way. Summative assessment can be used to answer the following questions:

- How well do children understand certain ideas/concepts?
- Can the children apply this understanding in other contexts?
- What level of attainment have the children reached?
- Are the children ready to move on to the next level?

Summative assessments have an importance that extends beyond the nursery/classroom in which they were made by providing information that is of use and interest to the whole school, the child's next school (in the case of transition) and the parents. One example of summative assessment is the use of Standard Assessment Tasks (SATs) that children take at the end of Key Stage 1. Schools can combine information from local and national SATs results with details of their own results to identify future targets for pupil achievement in the school. Although its primary purpose is not to inform the next step, the knowledge gained from summative assessment can be used in this way by subsequent teachers. An example of summative assessments being used formatively would be the use of reception teacher assessments by subsequent Year 1 teachers to inform their planning and preparation at the beginning of the year.

Summative assessment sheet

Name:
Date of birth:
Admission date:

English

AT1: Speaking and listening Comments	Rec.	Y1	Y2
Level 1			
Talks about matters of immediate interest			
Listens to others			
Responds appropriately			
Conveys simple meaning to range of listeners			
Speaks audibly			
Extends ideas and accounts by providing some detail			
Conveys/remembers a simple message			

Level 2	Rec.	Y1	Y2
Shows confidence when talking and listening			
Listens carefully			
Responds with increasing appropriateness to what others say			
Develops and explains ideas			
Speaks clearly and uses a growing vocabulary			
Includes relevant detail for needs of listener			
Conveys/remembers a more complex message			
Is aware of a more formal vocabulary and tone of voice			

Level 3	Rec.	Y1	Y2
Talks and listens confidently in different contexts			
Shows careful listening through relevant comment and questions			
Communicates and explores ideas in discussions, shows understanding of main points			
Adapts what they say to needs of listener varying use of vocabulary and level of detail			
Is aware of standard English and when it is used			

Summative assessments certainly have their uses as a measure of performance for children, their teachers and others. However, there can be limitations to some of these measurements. In the case of SATs, for example, they cannot hope to measure more than a small part of a child's overall capability. They need to be accompanied by broader, more holistic, views of pupils' achievements in the form of ongoing teacher assessments. A further limitation of summative assessment is its limited use in assisting teachers who are seeking to identify and respond to the learning needs of their pupils during the course of the year. To do this teachers need to engage in formative or diagnostic assessment.

Formative/diagnostic assessment

Assessment ought to take place on a regular basis, not just intermittently. It should be ongoing throughout the school year not just at the end of term, year or Key Stage. It is a continuous process which needs to be matched by a continuous recording process.

Formative assessment is used to inform the next stage in a child's learning. Its purpose is to recognize the achievements of a pupil so that these might be discussed and the appropriate next steps taken. Diagnostic assessment occurs when teachers seek to scrutinize and classify learning difficulties so that appropriate guidance can be given and intervention can take place. Formative assessment is about where the child has progressed to; diagnostic assessment looks at why a child is not progressing. Both inform the next step in terms of what the children should be learning and how to teach it. Formative (diagnostic) assessment can be used to answer the following questions:

- What do the children know/understand about a topic/subject?
- What do they know/understand about specific ideas/skills/procedures?
- Are any aspects of the topic causing problems for children?
- Can the children apply learning in new situations?
- Do the children hold any misconceptions?
- Is the pace and level of teaching set at appropriate levels?

Making formative/diagnostic assessments in the nursery/classroom

- Use systematic observation (watching, listening and talking to, the children) as one method of assessing formatively/diagnostically.
- A problem for teachers of young children is the small amount of time that they often get to spend with any one individual pupil and this can make diagnosis difficult. Keep examples of pupils' work as a source of concrete evidence to support some of your formative/diagnostic judgements based on observation.
- Assess a little bit at a time on a regular basis and use neutral or open-ended questions to get quality responses when working with young children.
- Review work with children in order to gain insight into processes as well as the products. It is easy to allow the focus of assessment to be on the outcomes of a lesson rather than the process. It is easier to make judgements about the accuracy of a piece of writing than it is to assess how it was produced, but for effective diagnosis you need to have some idea of both. Failure to diagnose difficulties accurately means that effective matching of tasks and differentiation is harder to do.
- Ask children to report on their progress and what they have done so far. Similarly, they can be questioned about how they completed an activity or accomplished a task.

Evaluative assessment

Assessment can be used to evaluate and influence policies and planning in a school or nursery on a wider scale than merely the subsequent planning by individual teachers. Such assessment is evaluative in nature. Evaluative assessment can be used to answer the following questions:

- Are the goals of the teaching programme appropriate for the pupils?
- How effective is the teaching programme in achieving these goals?

It is important to be clear about the relationship between assessment and evaluation. Evaluation involves making a judgement of some kind, possibly about the effectiveness or otherwise of a particular teaching programme. This judgement is based on the information obtained through assessment. Assessment provides a more valid base than the use of impression. The results of assessment therefore can be helpful in keeping track of the breadth and balance of the curriculum and in ensuring progression and continuity in children's learning as they move through the school from nursery and reception, to Key Stage 1 and on to Y3.

An evaluative assessment of reading materials

Mrs Wilson was appointed to the post of English coordinator in a primary school. Part of her responsibilities included monitoring and overseeing the loan of reading books to pupils for homework tasks. Parents were asked to help their children and the school by indicating in a report book what the children had read, how they had coped and what they thought of the stories. When Mrs Wilson reviewed the comments from parents she realized that they were strongly negative concerning the age, quality and content of the reading material. When Mrs Wilson spoke to children about the books available she discovered a reluctance to get involved in reading at home because the books were old, tatty and 'boring'. Mrs Wilson presented her assessment of the situation to her colleagues and the headteacher, who in turn discussed the matter with the governing body. The governors decided to make funds available for the school to buy new books for homework tasks and to release Mrs Wilson for two afternoons to organize the resources and loans system.

Methods of Assessment

When planning to assess children, teachers need to consider three questions:

1. What do I want to assess? (Do I want the pupils to demonstrate certain skills or am I trying to assess knowledge and understanding?)
2. How will I know if the children have achieved the learning objectives? (What will the children have to do or say to demonstrate attainment?)
3. How am I going to collect evidence for assessment? (This constitutes the assessment mode or method.)

Assessment modes could include

- systematic classroom observations (watching children's actions, listening to their conversation, listening to presentations such as reading out their stories, or question and answer sessions);
- making judgements based on outcomes (models, pieces of writing, drawings, paintings, number work); and
- making judgements against previous outcomes (stored examples of work from earlier pupils).

Systematic observation

Checking regularly that there is demonstrable progress in young children's learning can be achieved through systematic observation. Such observation is integral to work with young children and is essential for their continuous assessment. Observations can be both informal, such as watching children interacting with one another, and formal, such as structured observation to ascertain learning against a particular element of the National Curriculum Programmes of Study; they may involve the whole class, small groups, or individuals. Discussing activities with children might form part of a teacher's observation or could be conducted after an activity. Although the use of discussion between pupil and teacher as a method of assessment can be a time-consuming business, it is a very useful device for

- locating evidence of a child's success;
- diagnosing learning difficulties;
- monitoring progress over a period of time; and
- developing some insight into the ways in which a particular child learns and works.

Systematic observation, including discussion, provides a means by which children's knowledge and skills can be checked and explored through questioning and reporting back and can help to define more clearly any individual contributions to a group task. It is important to bear in mind that a child's response is not necessarily an accurate or reliable guide to knowledge and competence (SCAA, 1997), hence the need for a range of assessment techniques used in a variety of contexts over an extended period of time.

Assessing children in this way requires good classroom organization and management, particularly where teachers wish to assess a small group of individuals in situations where non-teaching support is limited or non-existent. Assessing through systematic observation requires attention and concentration. Teachers need to consider not only the child being assessed, but the rest of the children in the class.

The 'assessed' and the 'rest'

- How involved will you become in the activity itself? Too much involvement could make collecting the evidence difficult. Sitting too close to the children can make disengagement and note-taking almost impossible. Simultaneously teaching, listening, and making notes is not easy.
- How many children will you assess at any one time, and against how many learning objectives? It can be difficult to collect evidence for large numbers of children through observation and discussion. Likewise, trying to assess children against large numbers of learning objectives can become unmanageable. It is important to have a clear and uncomplicated set of objectives.
- Are the children aware of the purposes for both the task and the assessment? Explaining what you are going to be observing gives the children the chance to show if they know or can do it.
- Frequent interruptions will play havoc with your attempts to conduct assessments in the nursery/classroom. Yet young children are much more dependent upon their teachers than their older counterparts. It is important therefore to make maximum use of non-teaching support in the classroom and to plan low-intervention tasks for children where such support is limited or unavailable.

- It is important to remember too that assessment through systematic observation or discussion does not necessarily mean that you have to be with the children being assessed at all times. Planning which considers the balance between independent activity and teacher participation or group discussion may be a useful approach to take. For example, when assessing a group of children you could visit the group at regular intervals of time throughout an activity, you could visit the group at fixed points in the programme of activities, or you could work down a list of the children. Whichever option is chosen, it is important to ensure that there will be sufficient time to gather the necessary information without ignoring the needs of the rest of the class.

Observing nursery/reception pupils

Given the age and abilities of children between 3 and 5 years, many of the assessments that teachers make will be based on observations rather than on concrete pieces of work that the children have produced.

Assessing the youngest pupils using systematic observation

- Involve non-teaching colleagues in the process. Nursery nurses, non-teaching assistants and child-care assistants can all play an invaluable role in monitoring and reporting on young children's achievements and progress. Furthermore, given the importance of establishing a team approach to the teaching of young children, assessment that excludes all but the teacher from making judgements about children's learning is likely to undermine the team. The teacher cannot be everywhere at once and the involvement of the whole team under the guidance of the teacher makes the task of focusing on groups and individuals much more manageable in terms of creating time and opportunities to observe and talk with the children. All responsible staff have a contribution to make with the help of clip boards, post-it notes, and observation notebooks.
- Observations ought to be made on a broad front which reflects the breadth of the 3–5 curriculum; not just literacy and numeracy but also personal and social development, knowledge and understanding about the world, creative development and physical development.

Below are some examples of indicators that nursery/reception teachers might look for when assessing young children's progress and learning through systematic observation. The list should in no way be seen as comprehensive. Trainee and newly qualified teachers should refer to the further sources of information (p. 129) in order to extend their knowledge and understanding in this area.

Indicators to watch for

Possible indicators of achievement in personal and social development
The child can
- express feelings;
- communicate appropriately in social situations;
- initiate conversations with peers and adults;

- work cooperatively with peers;
- persevere when faced with a challenge; and
- cope effectively with changes in routines or staffing.

Possible indicators of achievement in language and literacy
The child can
- ask and answer questions;
- seek information;
- participate in discussions and imaginary play;
- respond appropriately to a speaker;
- demonstrate listening behaviour;
- recall experiences/retell stories;
- model (pretend) reading; select books;
- understand that text has meaning;
- recognize familiar signs, letters; and
- attempt own writing.

Possible indicators of achievement in mathematics
The child can
- form recognizable numbers and shapes;
- understand that mathematical symbols represent number and shape;
- understand and apply concepts such as behind, above, below, large, small;
- use number in everyday contexts;
- count and order;
- estimate and approximate; and
- measure and make judgements.

Possible indicators of achievement in knowledge and understanding about the world
The child can
- use five senses and ask questions about the world;
- suggest solutions to problems;
- demonstrate an awareness of cause and effect;
- predict consequences;
- make comparisons and identify similarities and differences;
- distinguish between living and non-living things;
- identify significant places in the locality (shops, mosque, post office);
- demonstrate an understanding of past, present and future;
- make things using tools and materials safely and effectively; and
- incorporate ICT into play situations.

Possible indicators of achievement in physical development
The child can
- move safely about the learning environment;
- participate in physical activities;
- use equipment safely and in a variety of ways;
- initiate own challenges;
- demonstrate hand-eye coordination and gross motor skills;
- demonstrate fine motor skills (manipulating scissors, pencils, construction materials);
- describe ways of keeping healthy; and
- describe ways of keeping safe.

Possible indicators of achievement in creative development
The child can
- use a range of responses in imaginary play;
- select materials for creative activities;
- participate in movement activities involving music;
- respond appropriately to different music (fast, slow, cheerful, sad);
- experiment with different art media; and
- demonstrate a rudimentary awareness of aesthetics, colour, shape and pattern.

Assessing outcomes

The concrete results of an activity can be a useful guide to learning, and small collections of children's work can illustrate their attainment very effectively. Such portfolios can provide a way of displaying a range of work, not simply written or number work but also project, ICT and creative work. Concrete outcomes assessed in conjunction with teacher–pupil discussions can be very helpful in enabling children to become more involved and take an active part in the process of assessment. This approach can help children to gain some insight into their own progress, strengths and weaknesses. It can also provide a useful starting point for setting targets for future learning. However, it is important to remember that concrete products alone may prove insufficient and inconclusive as evidence of attainment. It can be difficult to identify the features of a piece of work which indicate achievement and it may be necessary to support judgements made on the basis of outcomes with reference to either observations of the process or discussions of the work with the child. Many factors could influence the final outcome and lead teachers to misjudge children's learning. For example, where the collaborative setting actually belies the individual nature of the assessments being made, teachers will need to devise strategies for discerning individual contributions and comprehension.

Assessing
Writing Skills

and he went to The Shop with

his bicrtday mawny to buy

Some thing. He looked ot all

the Toys ^but he ^chose chotes a Little

cat. Just like Him. ✓

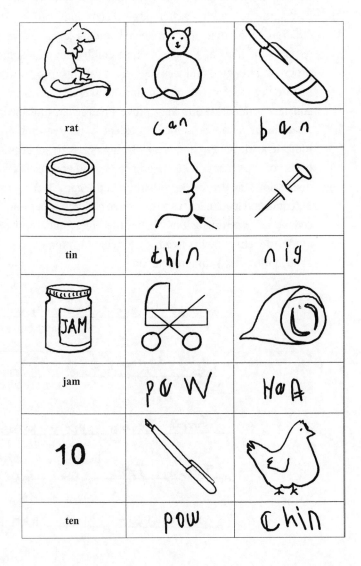

| Subject: English | | Date: 18.12.98 |

Subject: English   Date: 18.12.98

Class: 2   Year Group: 1

Work: Above Average   ☐
               Average   ☐
               Below Average   ☑

Focus: Word level work – onset and rhyme

Diagnostic Assessment: cannot always hear rhyme –
she was unable to write the cvc rhyming words even
with the pictures to help.

rat	c a n	b a n
tin	thin	n i g
jam	p o w	H o A
10		
ten	pow	chin

Benchmarking

When considering methods of assessing attainment through outcomes, teachers can also consider benchmarking. Benchmarking requires the teacher or the school to collect exemplar material (examples of other children's work) as a way of indicating the quality of work that should be expected at different levels from a particular group of children. Benchmarking not only acts as an aid to teachers in trying to determine the level of a particular piece of work, it can also provide pupils with insights into standards and expectations and can act as a spur to greater effort and higher achievement. The School Examination and Assessment Council publication *Children's Work Assessed* (1991) is one example of an attempt to introduce benchmarking on a national scale for Key Stage 1 pupils in the core curriculum areas of the National Curriculum. The SCAA's *Looking at Children's Learning* (1997) is a more recent attempt to provide similar guidance on the Desirable Outcomes.

Some principles of assessment

- Be clear about why you are assessing children. Enabling them to progress should have a high priority in these deliberations.
- Make sure the assessment allows pupils to demonstrate the appropriate skills, knowledge and/or attitudes.
- Assessment should not be limited to academic attainment alone. It should also provide information on progress in a child's development as an effective learner, including physical, social and emotional development.
- As far as possible, try to make assessment an integral part of teaching and learning in the nursery/classroom.
- Share the results of assessment with pupils and parents in order to improve confidence and motivation.
- Remember that parents can make a valuable contribution to assessment.
- Assess in ways that are ongoing as well as summative.
- Assess using a variety of methods depending on the needs and capabilities of the children. Assess in a variety of contexts depending on the nature of what is being assessed. This diversity will
    help to minimize possible bias in assessment;
    provide a more balanced picture of children's capabilities;
    help to allow for the age and level of pupils;
    take into account children whose first language is not English;
    be more sensitive to the sometimes different interests of boys and girls; and
    acknowledge the fact that the context in which assessment takes place can have a significant impact upon young children's performance.

Recording and Responding to the Results of Assessment

AUDIT

By the end of this section you should

- know about marking and monitoring children's work, providing constructive oral and written feedback, and setting targets for pupils' progress (Cb);
- know about different ways of recording children's progress systematically (Cc).

Giving constructive Feedback to Children

Discussions between teachers and pupils, including constructive feedback on their progress, take place every minute of every day in most nurseries and schools. Much of this feedback is informal in the sense that it constitutes part of the normal exchanges between children and adults. However, it is possible to institute more formal approaches by dedicating time to joint target-setting and self-appraisal/assessment by the children. Even very young children can get involved in self-reporting.

By utilizing their communication skills effectively teachers can do much to provide accurate, helpful and motivating feedback. It is not just a matter of what is communicated but also how. Teachers need to be aware of the non-verbal messages they give to children as well as the oral and written feedback that they provide. Their body language, facial expression and gestures can all be used to reinforce and emphasize the messages they give to children about their achievements and what they need to focus on in the future.

Marking is an important, and sometimes time-consuming, aspect of providing constructive feedback to children. Marking as children are working helps teachers to notice learning needs and to set learning targets in an ongoing fashion. However, in a classroom where there may be as many as 30 pupils it is unreasonable to expect the teacher to be marking everywhere at once. Furthermore, if teachers attempt to do all their marking in this way they may not leave themselves with any time to discuss pupils' attainment. As children get older and are able to cover increasing quantities of work, the task of marking as the lesson proceeds becomes increasingly difficult.

In some instances (where there are clear right and wrong answers) children can be encouraged to do some of their own marking. While there is always a danger that some children may adjust their answers to obtain perfect scores, their peers will normally alert the teacher to what is going on. In situations where judgements are more subjective, teachers will need to adopt an approach that is manageable, marking and assessing sufficient work during the lesson to ensure that encouragement and direction are possible, without trying to do everything and be everywhere at once. In such situations teachers need to make sure that they vary their focus to ensure that all the children experience this ongoing feedback on a regular basis even though they may not all receive it at the same time.

Feeding back to children orally and in writing

- Find something positive to say or write.
- Identify something for the child to work at (target setting).
- Try to use your feedback to help the children improve and develop.
- Set targets with the children at the start of an activity ('Today I want you to remember to use capital letters at the start of a sentence').
- Where some children are self-marking, do a few spot checks and keep reinforcing the message that only honest self-marking is of any value. Offer praise and recognition for honesty.
- Tell the rest of the class when a child has tried especially hard or been particularly successful (praising effort and achievement at the end of the lesson or day).

Recording

Recording young children's learning and experiences is an inevitable concomitant of assessment and evaluation. The scale of recording and reporting has greatly increased, largely in response to the demand for accountability rather than in recognition of the role it plays in the teaching and learning process. All schools and nurseries have to keep up-to-date records of children's progress and achievements. There is a great deal of guidance available to 3–8 teachers on recording systems but no universally imposed one. Although this approach has been beneficial in allowing for flexibility, it has also led some nurseries and schools to overestimate what is needed. Many 3–8 teachers spend considerable amounts of time trying to meet the requirements of unnecessarily complicated systems whose creation owes more to worries over increasing teacher accountability rather than to the need to inform teachers, pupils and others about children's progress.

Purposes of record keeping:

- informing future teaching (enables teachers to develop and evaluate their teaching programmes);
- ensuring that the school or nursery has an accurate and up-to-date profile of individual children's learning;
- providing the basis for reporting to parents and carers about the children's achievements and development;
- informing future teachers about a child's progress, needs, interests and capabilities, facilitating transition within and between schools;
- helping teachers to monitor pupil progress over time. Reveal patterns or problems and underpins summative statements;
- informing discussions with children on target setting; and
- providing evidence for a review of nursery/school policies and practices.

Collecting evidence

Records do not just involve the results of assessment and statements about attainment. They also need to include some evidence in support of these statements. This can be problematic for teachers working with young children where much of their learning and development could well be demonstrated outside the confines of the nursery/classroom, for example during a break time, while on a visit or in an assembly, and does not always result in a concrete product. A wide range of evidence increases the chances of making accurate judgements concerning the children's capabilities. A narrow range of learning approaches will lead to a more impoverished evidence base. This does not mean, however, that teachers need to start collecting everything; excessive amounts of evidence are likely to be unwieldy. Teachers should therefore provide sufficient evidence to back their judgements. A minimum amount of useful evidence should be the aim and 3–8 teachers will need to decide what to collect and how long to retain it.

Evidence collected ought to reflect the children's achievements and learning needs. It should arise from a broad range of activities. Young children can produce a wide range of concrete evidence on which teachers can give constructive feedback, including drawings or sketches, computer printouts, written work, graphs and charts, junk models, clay work, diagrams, paintings, diaries, plans and posters. Finally, evidence should be collected over an extended period of time, while simultaneously recognizing that some individual pieces of evidence may be superseded by subsequent examples. In other words, the evidence base needs to be reviewed from time-to-time.

Types of record

Plans

In part, some of the records kept by schools and nurseries will be formed by planning documents; these will provide information on the timing and content of topics that the children have experienced. Schemes of work and lesson/session plans are also a form of record, albeit of future intentions. Such whole school/nursery planning greatly reduces the need for individual teachers to spend time recording coverage of the curriculum. A session/lesson plan that has been modified or adjusted in the light of experience in order to better address the learning needs of the children forms a concrete record of how assessment has been used to inform future teaching.

Ticklists

Ticklists enable teachers to monitor those activities and elements of the curriculum that the children have experienced or completed. However, although they are relatively quick to use, a tick means only that a child has done something; it does not indicate the level of performance or achievement. Ticklists also have an additional problem in that they can become very long and unwieldy. They can be made more informative and have the capacity to record not just what has been covered but also the degree of success or achievement by using more than one symbol or by including a comments box.

Wordlist

	read	spell		read	spell		read	spell		read	spell
I			like			for			go		
going			a			come			big		
dad			went			she			can		
up			and			he			you		
they			am			day			my		
all			was			see			look		
on			is			are			away		
cat			the			mum			get		
of			it			we			at		
said			this			play			to		
dog			no			in			me		
yes											

Written comments

This form of record keeping has the added advantage of forming the basis of feedback to children. Making sure that you maintain sufficient mobility in the classroom to allow for marking and feedback sends an important message to the children about the importance of what they are doing. Marking helps teachers to monitor what the children have done and assess where they need to go next.

Notes

Many teachers use notebooks, clipboards or post-it notes to jot down incidents and observations. It is neither possible nor desirable to note down everything and teachers need to exercise their professional judgement as to what is useful to record and what is needless paperwork. It is also likely that the level of short-term recording that teachers do may well vary depending upon the pupils concerned.

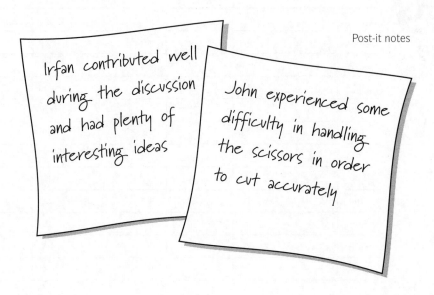

Post-it notes

Irfan contributed well during the discussion and had plenty of interesting ideas

John experienced some difficulty in handling the scissors in order to cut accurately

Portfolios

Examples of pupils' work, selected by the teacher, show children's achievements to date and can include information on National Curriculum levels and test results. Portfolios need to be reviewed and updated on a regular basis. Bin or send home outdated examples of children's achievements. Compiling portfolios is time-consuming for teachers and in some circumstances could constitute duplication especially where the children's workbooks contain much of this evidence already. Reviewing children's previous work contained in a portfolio can be an illuminating activity for both teachers and children and can provide graphic evidence of both progress and regression.

Records of Achievement and Experience

These are intended to be a child-centred approach to monitoring achievement in that the child selects the examples/evidence for inclusion, in discussion with the teacher. This approach is useful as a way of encouraging children to take greater responsibility for their own learning and get involved in self-assessment. Such records will not be restricted to school/nursery based achievements, but can also include successes beyond this context. However, as with portfolios, compiling records of achievement and experience can be a time-consuming process.

121

Record of Achievement and Experience

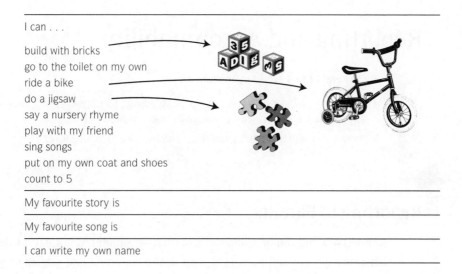

Reception

I like to . . .

I don't like to . . .

I know these colours

red
blue
yellow
purple
green
orange

I can draw this picture

I can . . .

build with bricks
go to the toilet on my own
ride a bike
do a jigsaw
say a nursery rhyme
play with my friend
sing songs
put on my own coat and shoes
count to 5

My favourite story is

My favourite song is

I can write my own name

Some principles of recording

Records should

- be kept up-to-date and be manageable for teachers, allowing information to be included and retrieved quickly and easily. It is impossible for any teacher to remember the details of observations and outcomes for any length of time, indeed it is possible to forget the detail of a child's remark by the end of a busy day, let alone a term. That said, recording everything is simply not practicable – teaching would grind to a halt. Good records are a compromise between what is informative and what is manageable.

They should

- show individual progress and achievements, and indicate areas for improvement;
- be accessible for all those using them, including colleagues, parents and other adults with a right to the information and, in the case of Primary Records of Achievement and Experience (PRAE), the pupils themselves;
- be ongoing and cumulative in nature, based on regular assessment in the form of systematic observations, discussions, directed tasks and tests;
- be linked to evidence which supports the judgements recorded;
- be used by future teachers. This may seem an obvious, not to say banal, statement. After all, it is clear that children ought not to be repeating things at the same level in subsequent classes. However, it is the case that some teachers like to form their own impressions of pupils and feel that others' records and evidence of past performance will colour their judgement. But subjective judgement is not eliminated by not looking at records and first impressions are no more reliable than any other impression. In addition, past performance ought to be the starting point for future teaching and learning. If teachers are not going to use the previous teacher's records it undermines the whole basis for keeping them.

Reporting and Accountability

By the end of this section you should

- know about the statutory assessment and reporting requirements and know how to prepare and present informative reports to parents (Cd);
- know about National Curriculum tests, and baseline assessment (Ci).

Reporting to Parents

In nurseries and infant schools where there is a high level of day-to-day contact between teachers and parents a great deal of informal and ongoing reporting is already taking place. In addition, every parent whose child is of statutory school age is entitled to an annual written report on their child's performance and achievement during the year. Reports have to contain brief particulars on the

122

child's achievements in the form of a series of short statements outlining successes and areas of weakness. The report should also contain information on a pupil's general educational progress which might include remarks on behaviour and attitude as well as academic attainment.

Annual Report to parents

Pupil name: *Shaida*   **School Year: 1998–99 (Reception)**

Language and literacy
Shaida always listens attentively and makes good contributions in class discussions. She loves reading and can read a range of texts independently. She is beginning to use a variety of strategies to tackle unfamiliar words and shows understanding of the main points of the book. Shaida is being encouraged to write at greater length and to extend her ideas. She can structure a simple story or account, and spell simple words correctly. Her handwriting is legible and she is working towards the more consistent use of upper and lower case letters.

Mathematics
Shaida has a good grasp of early number concepts in addition and subtraction to 20, and is developing mental recall of these facts. She has completed measurement activities involving length, weight and capacity and can use non-standard units. She can sort and classify objects and name and describe the properties of simple two-dimensional shapes. She can continue and make repeating patterns involving shape and colour with two changes.

Other areas of experience
In classroom tasks, Shaida has made observations, talked about her findings and made recordings of these in words and pictures. She can recognize similarities and differences in living things and objects, and demonstrates a good general knowledge. She draws, paints, cuts and makes with care and has plenty of ideas for her work. She shows good coordination when moving on the floor and apparatus during PE lessons. She likes to sing and can play percussion instruments.

Personal and social development
Shaida has made excellent progress in all curriculum areas, most notably in English and mathematics. She settles quickly to tasks, works hard and takes part in all areas of school life with growing confidence and a happy disposition. She is helpful and reliable and an asset to the class. I am sure that Shaida will continue to build on this super start. She is a pleasure to teach.

Number of attendances out of total number possible 300: 312

Number of unauthorised absences 0

This report may be discussed with . . . . on . . . .

at . . . .

Annual Report to parents

Pupil name: *Stephen*   **School Year: 1998–99 (Year 2)**

English

Stephen always listens attentively in class discussions, and he confidently makes thoughtful and interesting contributions. He continues to enjoy reading and can read a wide range of simple texts independently. He is developing the ability to use a range of strategies to read new words, and shows that he understands what he has read through oral questioning and comprehension exercises. He is always keen to write and puts real effort into his work. Stephen can develop his ideas for stories and accounts, and is working hard to use capital letters and full stops consistently, and to use descriptive language. He spells many words with regular spelling patterns correctly and is learning irregular words.

Mathematics

Stephen can use addition and subtraction when solving problems involving up to 20 plus objects. He has begun to understand the place value of each digit in a number and can use this to order numbers to 100. He has mental recall of number bonds to 20, and is developing this with higher numbers. He is working on early multiplication through continuous addition and counting on activities. He can use non-standard and some standard units to measure and order objects. Stephen has made data collections and recorded these in simple charts.

Science

He has completed science tasks about sound and light, forces, and plants. He can describe and name the simple features of objects, living things and events, and recognize similarities and differences. He can offer suggestions about how to find things out, has made predictions and tested his ideas. He asks and answers questions related to a task with interest. Stephen has made individual and group recordings of his work in a variety of ways including simple tables. He has an excellent general knowledge and is always eager to find out more.

Design and Technology

When designing and making Stephen can select from a range of materials and techniques and explain his choices. He has developed his skills in cutting, joining and assembling. He has made pictures and models to show his designs and can discuss his ideas and suggest improvements.

Information Technology

Stephen can recognize a range of IT equipment and has learned to control and operate different devices. He has used the computer to communicate in pictures and text and learned more about using the keyboard and the mouse.

History

Stephen can recognize changes in his own and others' lives and use related vocabulary to describe the passing of time. He has used objects, books and photographs to find out more about the past, and can sequence objects and events into simple chronological order.

Geography

He has made observations and recordings about the features of the local environment – the types and uses of buildings and land, and the people and their roles. He has talked about attractive and unattractive features and made simple plans and routes.

Art

Stephen has worked practically and imaginatively with materials, tools and techniques to create pieces of art work. He is developing his use of colour, pattern and texture, and takes care in observational work.

Music

He has learned songs and rhymes, and is an excellent singer who confidently performs on his own. He has learned to name and play simple percussion instruments, and to explore and select sounds to express ideas.

Physical Education

Stephen is well coordinated and moves confidently on the floor and apparatus during PE lessons. He has developed and refined his skills in using small apparatus, and works enthusiastically in games.

Religious Education

Stephen has listened to Bible stories and learned about the life of Jesus and the work of the church. He always shows care and concern for others, and has a responsible and reliable attitude.

General Comments

Stephen approaches all his work with enthusiasm and a desire to do well. He has made very good progress in his work across all areas of the curriculum. He is a happy, friendly member of the class who has been a pleasure to teach. Thank you for your home support which, coupled with Stephen's hard work, will ensure his continuing success.

Number of attendances out of total number possible 302: 312

Number of unauthorized absences 0

This report may be discussed with . . . . on . . . .

at . . . .

Reporting on Baseline Assessment

Prior to 2000 baseline assessments were normally conducted within the first half-term of a child entering the reception class. With the introduction of the Foundation Stage in 3–8 education, incorporating nursery and reception years, these assessments will be conducted towards the end of the reception year in preparation for the start of Key Stage 1. In such a situation baseline assessment will

- form both a summative record of pupil attainment and a formative and diagnostic tool for future Year 1 teachers;
- provide information that is useful to a school as a whole in helping it to plan and manage its provision in terms of curriculum and resources; and
- provide a benchmark against which a school can make judgements on the extent of a pupil's progress at the end of Key Stage 1.

Baseline assessment seeks to identify the strengths and learning needs of individual children, to enable teachers to plan appropriate teaching and learning activities to meet these needs and to inform discussions with parents and future teachers on progress and performance. Opportunities for structured dialogue between parents and schools on pupils' progress against these baseline assessments can take place at various intervals during the child's time in school. As with initial pupil assessments in nursery, collaboration with parents and carers is an important part of baseline assessment as it assists parents in becoming familiar with the nature and purpose of assessment. It is also an opportunity for them to provide information which might contribute to the assessment. Parents and carers, after all, have a considerable amount of knowledge about their children which can be invaluable in helping teachers build up a more complete picture of a pupil.

Although baseline assessments lean heavily towards literacy and numeracy, they are also expected to take into account the wider curriculum. They can be conducted both through teacher observations and/or focused assessment tasks. The approaches used by schools when making and recording baseline assessments include criterion-referencing, key skills checklists, and descriptive or narrative statements. Manageability is a key feature as many reception classes have more than one intake during a year and include rising-5 pupils (children who will reach the age of 5 in the coming term). Recording and conducting baseline assessments in such a changing environment therefore is heavily influenced by the perceived benefit to the teacher, the extent of the paperwork involved, the numbers, ages and full-time/part-time status of the children, and the amount and quality of non-teaching classroom support available.

Entry/Baseline assessment example

	Nurs. 1	Nurs. 2	Baseline	KS1	TA
Age					
Date of assessment					
Mathematics					
Ma1 Using and Applying					
A yet to develop/be observed					
B matches simple objects					
C sorts using own attribute(s)					
D uses equipment and maths knowledge to solve a task, with help					

E decides how to tackle a task and talks about what she/he has found using mathematics as an integral part of activities			
F tackles a more complex task (e.g. including simple addition). (Level 1)			
Ma2 Number			
A yet to develop/be observed			
B can say numbers to at least 5			
C uses counting equipment; counts sets !:1 to at least 5			
D recognizes numbers 1–10/counts and orders to 10			
E performs 3 simple additions (to 10) with support; writes numbers 1–10			
F counts/orders/adds/subtracts numbers in problems involving at least ten objects. (Level 1)			

(Nottinghamshire County Council, 1998)

Reporting to parents on Standard Assessment Tasks (SATs)

All Y2 pupils must undertake SATs during their final term of Key Stage 1, during which time they will be assessed against level descriptions contained in the National Curriculum Attainment Targets. The final overall results of these tasks on a school level will be made public, but only teachers, parents and pupils see the detailed results for individual children. Schools are expected to report annually to parents on the SATs results, and teacher assessments (based on the same level descriptions) are reported alongside the test results. Where there is a discrepancy between what a teacher says about a child's achievements as a result of teacher assessment, and what the child has achieved in the SAT, it is the SAT result that is preferred. This is interesting and worth noting because for many people formal assessments, particularly public examinations or tasks such as SATs, are seen as being more objective than the judgements and critical appraisal made by individual teachers. It is also worth noting that the concept of objectivity is something of an illusion in that the mere fact that an assessment is universal does not eliminate bias. Since SATs are not compiled in a vacuum there must be an inevitable element of bias. SATs may be valid in that they assess what they say they are assessing, and they may be reliable in that they offer consistency of results over different activities and times, but that is not the same as saying that they are objective and hence should be given primacy over teacher assessments.

Moderation meetings, at which teachers attempt to reach a shared understanding about standards through pupil profiles, samples of work, and SAT results are important in trying to ensure fairness and a degree of comparability across the system. They also constitute another example of reporting, this time to fellow professionals. Such comparability is essential if any summative or evaluative statements are to be made concerning the SAT results locally, regionally or nationally.

In many ways SATs are a product of the tensions inherent in a system which is seeking to measure children's performance to support the teaching and learning process while at the same time measuring that performance as a way of ensuring teacher accountability. The Task Group on Assessment and Testing (TGAT) was formed to propose a 'national assessment system which enhances teaching and learning without any increase in the calls on teachers' and pupils' time for activities which directly promote learning' (TGAT, 1988). The manageability of assessment is crucial, and the need for it often results in compromises over validity, reliability and objectivity. The original assessments envisaged in the TGAT report of 1988 would have given comprehensive insights into children's learning but were too time-consuming and unmanageable given the resources of staff and time in many infant schools. Consequently, the SATs are more manageable, but equally much less useful, from the point of view of either identifying learning needs for the next Key Stage, or adequately and comprehensively measuring performance across the whole curriculum for accountability purposes. Furthermore, in a climate featuring high levels of teacher accountability, assessments such as the SATs can skew the curriculum and the teacher's efforts away from education and towards passing the test, sometimes undermining the professionals' capacity to determine children's achievement and potential in the process. SATs are inherently reductionist. They offer useful comparisons to teachers, but across a fairly narrow front.

Some principles of reporting and accountability

When reporting on pupil attainment
• make reference to children's achievements in relation to Desirable Outcomes/Early Learning Goals or National Curriculum level descriptions;
• include some description of children's achievements in relation to the wider curriculum;
• suggest areas and ways in which children can improve on their attainment to date;
• begin your comments by referring to positive factors and ensure any subsequent criticism is constructive in nature;

128

- maintain a professional commitment to confidentiality;
- value the contribution made by pupils and parents in assessment and recording; and
- use methods that are manageable and understandable for all involved.

FURTHER SOURCES OF INFORMATION

Monitoring and Assessing 3–8 Pupils

Ackers, J. (1994) '"Why involve me?" Encouraging children and their parents to partcipate in the assessment process', in L. Abbott and R. Rodger (1994) *Quality Education in the Early Years*. Buckingham: Open University Press.

School Curriculum and Assessment Authority (1995) *Consistency in Teacher Assessment: Guidance for Schools, Key Stages 1 to 3*. London: SCAA.

School Curriculum and Assessment Authority (1997) *Looking at Children's Learning*. London: SCAA.

School Examinations and Assessment Council (1991) *Children's Work Assessed*. London: SEAC.

Recording and Responding to the Results of Assessment

Dean, J. (1993) *Organising Learning in the Primary School Classroom, 3rd edition*. London: Croom Helm.

Qualifications and Curriculum Authority (1999) *Keeping Track: Effective Ways of Recording Pupil Achievement to Help Raise Standards*. London: QCA.

Reporting and Accountability

Qualifications and Curriculum Authority (1999) *Keeping Track: Effective Ways of Recording Pupil Achievement to Help Raise Standards*. London: QCA.

School Curriculum and Assessment Authority (1997) *Looking at Children's Learning*. London: SCAA.

School Examinations and Assessment Council (1991) *Children's Work Assessed: Key Stage 1*. London: SEAC.

Sharman, C., Cross, W. and Vennis, D. (1995) *Observing Children: A Practical Guide*. London: Cassell.

Other Professional Requirements

SUMMARY

Teaching young children requires a degree of familiarity with the legislation and systems governing teacher's actions, as well as being able to make use of inspection and research evidence to inform and improve teaching. Teachers need to be able to deal with some of the uncertainties of teaching and be ready, able and willing to continue to learn from experience, adapting and improving their practice to increase both their competence and their confidence. Teaching is about much more than the competences, such as the mechanics of planning a lesson or organizing a display board. Teaching is a profession, not just a job, and as such its members are subject to certain professional standards, expectations and codes of conduct outlined in Section D of the Standards for Initial Teacher Training.

By the end of this chapter you should know about

- the extent of the duties of the 3–8 teacher (Dai);
- the teacher's legal liabilities and responsibilities (Daii);
- the need to establish effective working relationships with parents, pupils, colleagues and others (Db,d,g);
- the need for high standards of personal and professional conduct, including taking responsibility for your own professional development (Dc,e);
- the development of whole-school policies and practices (Df); and
- the structure and function of governing bodies, including their role during OFSTED inspections (Dh).

The Responsibilities of the 3–8 Teacher

AUDIT

By the end of this section you should

- have a working knowledge and understanding of teachers' professional duties as set out in the current School Teachers' Pay and Conditions document, issued under the School Teachers' Pay and Conditions Act 1991 (Dai).

The School Teachers' Pay and Conditions Act 1991

The School Teachers' Pay and Conditions Act 1991 sets out the pay and conditions of teachers in England and Wales. The tasks of 3–8 teachers are many and include a wide range of professional duties in common with those of all other teachers. The Act provides for the constitution of a Review Body and defines the powers and responsibilities of the Secretary of State for Education and Employment to make Statutory Orders on teachers' pay and conditions.

The function of the Review Body is to consider matters relating to pay and conditions and to report their findings and recommendations to the Secretary of State. It is intended as a way of trying to ensure a rational basis for policy-making based on balanced consideration of the evidence. Not only may the Review Body consider issues for itself, but the Secretary of State may also ask it to examine a particular matter and report back within a given period. In such cases those affected – teachers, their unions, school governors and Local Education Authorities – have to be given the opportunity to submit evidence to the Review Body. Once the Secretary of State has received the report and advice from the Review Body there is a legal requirement to publish the report and subsequently seek to make a Statutory Order based on that report. In so doing, the Secretary of State has the power to modify or change the recommendations. Although the Secretary of State has the power to override and ignore the Review Body, to do so completely could prove politically embarrassing. In addition to seeking recommendations from the Review Body, the Secretary of State also has the power to make Statutory Orders in his/her own right. Whenever a Statutory Order is made, teachers must be paid according to the pay scales laid down in it, and any conditions set out in the Statutory Order become part of teachers' contracts.

Pay

Teachers' salaries are determined by the number of points a member of staff has reached on a pay spine. These points will be assessed and awarded by a local education authority if a teacher is employed centrally or if the school or nursery at which they are employed does not have a delegated budget. Where a school does have a delegated budget, or in the case of grant-maintained schools, it is the governing body's responsibility to make the points assessment. If trainee or newly qualified teachers are uncertain as to their points entitlement, their teaching unions will be able to offer advice.

Points awarded in 1999

- Newly qualified teachers with first- or second-class honours degrees or higher degrees were entitled to two points.
- An additional point was added for every year's experience gained for the first seven years of service in the case of graduates with good honours degrees, and 9 years for those without. Spine point 9 was the maximum point which a teacher could reach by virtue of experience and qualifications alone. This yearly increment was not automatic and could be withheld by the LEA or governing body if they felt that a teacher's performance was not satisfactory.
- Many teachers are expected to take on posts of responsibility during their teaching careers and some of these posts could also carry additional points, for example English Coordinator, Nursery Team Leader, Key Stage 1 Coordinator.
- LEAs and governing bodies could award extra points where recruitment and retention was difficult (in certain parts of the country and in certain subject areas) and in cases of excellence.
- Teachers who were primarily engaged in teaching children with Special Educational Needs were entitled to an extra point on the pay scale and could receive two such points should the governors so decide.

(NUT, 1998b)

Conditions of service

Under the terms of the 1991 Act all teachers must carry out their professional duties as well as any particular duties that can be reasonably assigned to them by the headteacher. The term *reasonable* will appear repeatedly in this chapter in relation to teachers' duties and responsibilities. As you will see, it is invariably open to interpretation.

Teachers employed on a full-time basis are expected to work for 195 days (a total of 1265 hours) during the school year. Five of these days are allocated for staff and curriculum development. In addition to the 1265 figure, teachers are required to work any additional hours needed to enable them to discharge their professional duties effectively. These additional hours would normally be taken up by tasks such as report writing, attending staff meetings and, of course, planning, preparation and marking.

- Teachers are expected to promote the well-being of individual children and alongside this to maintain good order and discipline in the classroom.
- They must safeguard the health and safety of the children in their care, both in school and on outside visits.
- Teachers are expected to take part in activities such as registration, playground supervision and attending assemblies.
- During teaching, staff must ensure that lessons are properly planned. They must also be prepared to take part in medium-term planning and preparation, and whole-school approaches to the curriculum. This planning and teaching must take individual needs and abilities into account.
- Staff must also engage in assessing and reporting on children's progress and attainment, for example recording and reporting on the personal and social needs of children, liaising with parents and working with outside agencies and individuals such as Special Needs colleagues. For teachers of Y2 pupils, this would also include participating in arrangements for SATs, while in reception it would mean undertaking baseline assessments.
- Beyond the classroom, teachers of young children are required to take part in appraisal activities aimed at improving their own professional competence and as part of this, to review, from time to time, their current practice and their training and development needs.
- Participation at staff meetings and in-service training days is mandatory.
- Teachers can also be asked to take part in the selection and recruitment of new staff, mentoring newly qualified colleagues and taking responsibilities across the school for coordinating a curriculum area, which would involve ordering resources, developing documentation and supporting the staff development of colleagues.

The rest of this chapter will deal in more detail with some of the regulations governing many of these key duties and offer suggestions on good practice and further reading. School Teachers' Pay and Conditions of Employment 1999 (Circular 12/99) is on the DfEE website (www.dfee.gov.uk).

Legislation Relating to Equality of Opportunity

By the end of this section you should

- have a working knowledge and understanding of teachers' legal liabilities and responsibilities relating to the Race Relations Act 1976 and the Sex Discrimination Act 1975 (Daii).

134

Teaching in a Multi-cultural Society

The Race Relations Act (1976) makes direct or indirect discrimination on the grounds of race, colour, ethnic or national origins illegal. Discriminatory behaviour must be opposed by teachers as it creates barriers and obstacles that disadvantage and exclude children.

- **Direct discrimination** is considered to have occurred in any instance where an individual is overtly treated unfavourably.
- **Indirect discrimination** relates to those instances where individuals are ostensibly being treated equally, but where the outcome is actually discriminatory in nature. Indirect discrimination through a school's/nursery's admissions policies for example is unlawful.

(Equal Opportunities Commission, 1982)

Section 71 of the Act places an onus upon schools to work actively towards the elimination of racial discrimination and the promotion of equal opportunities and positive relations between staff, pupils and parents of different racial groups. Trainee and newly qualified teachers wishing to explore this aspect of their role further may wish to visit the Comission for Racial Equality's website, (www.cre.gov.uk).

Although the 1976 Race Relations Act seeks to end racial discrimination it does provide for the particular needs of certain groups in society to be met. Ending discrimination should not be equated with treating every child as identical. Dietary and clothing requirements need to be respected, as do religious holidays and festivals. Assemblies provide a valuable opportunity to impart anti-racist values to young children, as do projects and topics such as 'Ourselves' which offer opportunities to raise children's awareness of diversity in society, although teachers need to be careful to avoid tokenistic approaches. Staff need to be alert to instances where large numbers of ethnic minority children are located in lower ability groups and to look for ways to tackle this 'underachievement'. At the same time, every parent needs to be able to understand school documents: booklets, letters, signs, displays, records and reports. Resources, such as reading and reference books, ought to be chosen carefully so as to avoid racist stereotyping. Some education authorities have within them centres and organizations such as Development Education Centres which can be an excellent source of multi-cultural and anti-racist resources covering the whole curriculum. Although the facilities and materials available at such centres vary quite considerably due to differences in funding, trainee and newly qualified teachers would be well advised to find out if such a centre exists in their region and to contact it for resources and advice.

Developing a multi-cultural/anti-racist approach in the nursery/classroom

- Spell and pronounce children's names properly.
- Help children to recognize and challenge discriminatory practices and behaviour.
- Help children to begin to understand ideas such as fairness, justice and diversity.

- Guide children in the adoption and use of non-discriminatory language.
- Praise and reinforce non-discriminatory behaviour in children.
- Tackle discriminatory behaviour head-on.
- Demonstrate that you value and respect diversity and individual differences by using pupils' first language where possible and by showing respect for traditions, cultures and protocols.
- Acquire and share knowledge about the historical, cultural and spiritual backgrounds in the local community.
- Enable children to take part in the everyday activities of their local community.

Equality of Opportunity for Boys and Girls

Equality of access

John and Helen (Y1) were asked to produce a piece of writing on the computer. The teacher noticed that John had occupied the seat in front of the keyboard and was monopolizing the activity. The teacher intervened and informed John that it was a joint task and that Helen needed to have a go on the computer too. The teacher then moved on to work with another group of children. John meanwhile sat back in his seat with his arms folded. Helen had to reach across him to get to the keyboard. Before long Helen's exclusion was reimposed.

Like the 1976 Race Relations Act, the 1975 Sex Discrimination Act makes discrimination on the grounds of sex illegal. Also, like racial discrimination, sex discrimination is identified as being either direct or indirect in nature and both are prohibited. Schools and nurseries must provide an entitlement curriculum for both boys and girls. In part, providing an entitlement curriculum for both sexes concerns access; for example, girls have an equal entitlement to experience with the computers and construction kits. However, promoting equality of opportunity for both boys and girls also means addressing the expectations and attitudes that some pupils have acquired. Young children can form strong opinions about boys' things and girls' things at a very early age and as they get older these attitudes often are linked to job aspirations and life choices in a very limiting way.

Tackling attitudes

A newly qualified teacher working with a class of Y2 children had planned a simple design and technology activity involving textiles in which the children would be asked to design and make some clothes for a doll. During a discussion with the headteacher about resources, the headteacher cautioned her that some of the boys were likely to be extremely hostile to the idea of any work involving dolls, textiles and sewing, as this would be seen as a girls' activity. After discussing strategies with the headteacher the NQT asked the children to make papier mâché models of themselves. The children were then asked to make clothes for these figures. The boys did not perceive their models as dolls and were enthusiastic about working with the textiles and sewing materials.

Promoting equality of opportunity for boys and girls in the nursery/classroom

- Give frequent, positive and encouraging feedback to both boys and girls across the curriculum.
- Have high expectations of girls as well as boys across the curriculum.
- Teach the children that certain subjects and areas of learning are not the preserve of one sex.
- Encourage the use of non-sexist language and procedures. Do girls always 'clear up'?
- Provide a variety of learning materials and ensure that girls and boys have opportunities to develop their skills and confidence in using these materials through hands-on experience.
- Remember that, at times, equality of access will require active intervention. It is important to be aware of how boys and girls interact in lessons and where necessary tackle the behaviour of some of the boys. Such behaviour could include calling out while girls put their hands up, ridiculing wrong answers, groaning at correct answers, playing in an aggressive manner, and pushing other pupils, including girls, out of reach of equipment and resources.
- Challenge gender stereotypes of the sort sometimes found in books and other resources by promoting positive images of women and men.
- Evaluate and reflect upon your teacher/pupil interactions. Do you give equal amounts of time to boys and girls? Do you respond to boys and girls differently? Are boys *challenged* and girls *helped*?
- Seek to raise and broaden parental expectations of both boys and girls.

Ensuring the Health and Safety of Young Children

By the end of this section you should

- have a working knowledge and understanding of Section 7 and Section 8 of the Health and Safety at Work Act 1974; and teachers' common law duty to ensure that pupils are healthy and safe on school premises and when leading activities off the school site, such as educational visits, school outings or field trips (Daii).

In loco parentis

All teachers have a common law duty to take good care of their pupils. Being *in loco parentis* must rank very highly on a teacher's list of priorities. It is particularly fundamental for teachers of the youngest, 3–8, pupils. As child experts, teachers are presumed to be familiar with the likely actions of their pupils in a given situation and are expected to be able to exercise a degree of foresight. Teachers who fail to prevent injury or harm to a child in their care when the risks could be reasonably foreseen are themselves in danger of being deemed negligent. Unfortunately, exact definitions of what constitutes such negligence do not exist and instead, where accusations of negligence arise, the final judgements are likely to be made on the facts of the case. Teachers of young children therefore need to make every effort to ensure their children's safety and not expose pupils to unnecessary hazards.

A major problem for teachers trying to exercise this foresight is that no environment, and certainly no 3–8 setting, can be made entirely risk free. Young children will always fall over, bump their heads, or trap their fingers from time to time. The only way to prevent all these accidents in schools and nurseries would be to close them. This is clearly a nonsense, indeed risk management and risk awareness are important skills for children to acquire given that they cannot be supervised 24 hours a day. Consequently, teachers need to reduce the risks to acceptable levels by organizing and maintaining a safe learning environment in the nursery/classroom (see Chapter 2) and by thinking carefully about the children in their care.

Thinking about the children

- Are they mature enough and dexterous enough to handle certain tools and materials?
- Are they strong enough to move certain objects?
- To what extent can they take responsibility for themselves and their actions?
- Do they have any physical disabilities that might put them at risk?
- Are nursery/school rules and conventions (e.g. no running) clearly understood?

Health and Safety at Work

In addition to teachers' common law duty to care for their pupils, they are also bound by the provisions of the Health and Safety at Work Act 1974. Under the provisions of this Act all employees, including teachers of young children, must not meddle or interfere with anything provided for the purpose of ensuring people's health and safety. They must also have a care for their own safety at work and the safety of others who might be affected by either their actions or their failure to act. Teachers are required to cooperate with others who have duties under the Act such as the school/nursery health and safety representative and the first aid specialist; failure to do this could lead to disciplinary action or even dismissal. Schools and nurseries have health and safety policies (often based on LEA policies) and staff are expected to be familiar with them.

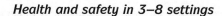
Responsibilities of the headteacher

The headteacher must

- ensure that all staff receive instruction in their duties regarding health and safety matters;
- ensure that all staff are adequately trained to carry out their duties;
- fully understand the school's fire drill procedures; and
- check the nursery/school on a regular basis for health and safety issues.

Responsibilities of teaching and non-teaching staff

- All staff, teaching and non-teaching, must be familiar with the school's health and safety policy, the implications of that policy and any procedures, arrangements and practices relating to it.
- All employees, pupils and others must receive appropriate instruction to enable them to operate in a safe and efficient manner (for example, fire drills).
- All staff must report to the headteacher any problems, defects or hazards that are brought to their notice.

Responsibilities of the caretaker

- The caretaker is responsible for ensuring that cleaning staff are adequately informed, instructed and trained in the safe use and storage of equipment, cleaning substances and other materials.
- The caretaker must not use, or allow cleaning staff to use, unsafe equipment.

Educational Visits

Trips and visits can be a wonderful stimulus for teaching and learning across the curriculum. Using the environment makes a contribution to the intellectual and practical development of pupils as individuals and as informed members of society. Educationally, outside visits offer real opportunities for community inter-action and for linking nursery and school experiences with the wider world, enabling young children to become more aware of the diversity of people, places and objects. There are however, major implications in terms of health and safety for the teacher. Educational visits will test a teacher's relationships, control and organization. Teachers who fail to encourage their children to exhibit responsible behaviour in the nursery or classroom can hardly expect them to suddenly exhibit it on the local bus. Outside the school gates, the children are beyond their normal closed environment and consequently they are not so easily observed, not as easily held accountable and are subjected to wider influences. In this looser context it is not as easy for teachers to exercise control; lack of control carries with it potential risks to the health and safety of the children.

Preparation can greatly increase the chances of a safe and successful visit. Local walks can give young children useful training in crossing roads, public behaviour, and staying with designated adults. Such walks provide teachers with good opportunities for making it clear to the children that in the outside world the standards of behaviour expected are even more rigorous than those in school or nursery. Ensuring good behaviour is not just a method of preserving the teacher's sanity, it is a prerequisite for safety and learning. Teachers of young children should always conduct a risk assessment prior to a class visit. It is important to bear in mind the need to give consideration to *likelihood* as well as *severity*, and to be prepared to deal with any accidents should they occur.

Reception/Y1 visit to the local park

Risk	Severity	Likelihood	Action
Small brook running through the park, danger of pupils falling in.	Water very shallow – low.	Medium to high.	Pack spare clothes, allocate specific children to specific adults for better supervision and brief adult helpers as to the risk.
Dogs off the lead.	Potentially high.	Medium to high.	Talk to children prior to visit about not approaching strange dogs, suggest strategies such as ignoring animals and staying with adults. Alert adult helpers.

A well organized and executed visit can inspire and enthuse young children and the momentum can last for quite some time. A poorly organized and riotous visit endangers the children and could rebound on the nursery/school, and hence on the teacher in charge. Here are some suggestions of things to consider before taking young children on walks and visits.

The children

- Do any of the children have a medical condition such as epilepsy or asthma which needs to be taken into account?
- Do any of them suffer from travel sickness and if so, do their parents give them medication prior to journeys?
- Have the children been told where they are going, who with, why and what's expected?
- How will they remember and/or record their experiences?

Know your pupils

A student teacher arranged a visit to the local canal, situated approximately three-quarters of a mile from the school. There were 30 Y1/2 pupils in the class, one of whom suffered from arthritis. The student teacher had not fully appreciated the child's condition. Half way to the canal it became clear that the child was experiencing some discomfort and that if the walk continued this discomfort could become more serious. The student teacher gave the child a piggyback ride all the way there and all the way back rather than abort the visit for the whole class. Not surprisingly this was not an ideal solution. Other children wondered why they could not have a ride too and, by the time they returned to the school, the student teacher also was unwell.

The parents/adult helpers

- No child can be taken out of nursery/school without the parents' permission. Letters therefore need to be sent to parents informing them of the details of the visit such as appropriate clothing, date, time and cost.
- Accompanying parents should be briefed as to what is being asked of them. Which children are they to accompany? What should they wear? Why are the children going, and what are the (learning) purposes of the visit?
- Make sure that there are enough adults to supervise the children adequately (3 to 1 in nursery and 6 to 1 with infants are the optimum ratios).

The site

- Wherever possible teachers should check the site before setting out with the children. This may be done in person or, in the case of more distant locations, by telephone. Even if the teacher has been to the site in previous years, things change.
- Where will the children eat, sit, keep dry, go to the toilet?
- Are there any particular hazards to avoid?
- What are the procedures in the event of an emergency, for example a fire alarm?

Check the details

A student teacher arranged a whole day visit to a zoo in the next county for two reception classes. The school hired two coaches, parents were recruited and the headteacher decided to accompany the party. The children were prepared for the visit and, in particular, for the reptile house which was the main focus of the trip. When the coaches arrived at the zoo they were informed that the reptile house was closed that day and that, had the student teacher contacted the zoo beforehand about the visit, they could have informed her of this fact.

The route

- On local visits it is advisable to check the route. What are the safest crossing points, and are there any toilets *en route* just in case?
- Are you familiar with details such as bus times, stopping places and alternative buses in the event of a non-arrival. In some areas it is necessary to ring the bus company beforehand to inform them of the trip; failure to do so could mean drivers refusing to take the party on board.

- Careful and responsible supervision, combined with good preparation, will do much to reduce the risk of emergencies. However, a small first aid kit for cuts and grazes can be very useful.
- Sick bags are essential if using road transport.
- Spare clothes are a good idea if travelling anywhere near water.

142

Children's Welfare

By the end of this section you should

- have a working knowledge and understanding of teachers' legal liabilities and responsibilities relating to the promotion of children's welfare (Section 3(5) of the Children Act 1989), the role of the education service in protecting children from abuse (DfEE Circular 10/95), and appropriate physical contact with pupils (DfEE Circular 10/95) (Daii);
- know about the importance of developing effective working relationships with professional colleagues including, where applicable, associate staff (Db).

The Children Act 1989 and Circular 10/95

Under the 1989 Children Act, schools and their local education authorities are required to assist their local social services departments when those departments are investigating allegations of child abuse. Individual teachers in schools are expected to do what is reasonable in the circumstances to safeguard and promote the welfare of their pupils. Once again, as with the common law duty of care, there is no exact definition of what constitutes reasonable. More recently, Circular 10/95 Protecting Children from Abuse (DfEE, 1995) attempted to assist teachers in fulfilling their responsibilities to their pupils under the provisions of the 1989 Act by clarifying what was expected.

The main points arising from Circular 10/95 are as outlined below

- All staff should be alert to signs of abuse and know to whom they should report any concerns or suspicions.
- All schools and colleges should have a designated member of staff responsible for coordination of action within the institution and liaison with other agencies including the Area Child Protection Committee (ACPC).
- All schools and colleges should be aware of the child protection procedures established by the ACPC and, in the case of LEA maintained schools, by the local education authority.
- All schools and colleges should have procedures (of which all staff should be aware) for handling suspected cases of abuse of pupils or students, including procedures to be followed if a member of staff is accused of abuse. Schools' and colleges' procedures should

be consistent with those of the ACPC and, in the case of LEA maintained schools, with those of the local education authority.

- Guidelines about procedures to be followed if a member of staff is accused of abuse have been drawn up by the Council of Local Education Authorities and the six teacher unions. A copy has been annexed to the Circular.
- Staff with designated responsibility for child protection should receive appropriate training.
- Schools should develop a child protection policy and make it known to parents.
- In every local education authority there should be a senior officer with responsibility for coordinating action on child protection across the authority.

(DfEE, October 1995, Summary)

The main point for students on 3–8 teacher training courses and newly qualified teachers arising from the 1989 Act and Circular 10/95, is that should they suspect a child is being abused, then they must alert the designated member of staff in the school whose role it is to liaise with the various child protection agencies. Students and teachers can obtain a copy of the full Circular and its annexes by telephoning the Department for Education and Employment.

Identifying Abuse

Abuse may take a number of forms (Kay, 1999).

- **Physical abuse**
A child may suffer actual injuries as a result of the violent actions of others. The results can include tell-tale marks such as cuts, bruises and burns.

- **Physical neglect**
A child's suffering is the result of inaction and a failure to protect, care properly and attend to physical needs.

- **Sexual abuse**
Children are exploited sexually by adults. This is a particularly emotive subject and may result in children being noticeably withdrawn or, paradoxically, highly precocious.

- **Emotional abuse**
This abuse is not physical in nature and may not leave any visible marks, but it is no less harmful to a young child. Emotional abuse can result in children being persistently ill-treated or rejected by those whose duty it is to care for them. It can produce profoundly damaging effects on the emotional and behavioural development of the child, resulting in excessive 'clinginess' or aggression in the nursery/school.

Simply because a young child is behaving aggressively or appears withdrawn does not constitute evidence of abuse or neglect of any kind. However, it could be an indicator and teachers of young children need to be alert for the signs, and if necessary try to elicit some information from the child in a tactful, sympathetic and non-leading fashion. Any such discussion must be handled very carefully. Under no circumstances should trainee teachers initiate such a discussion without first referring to their class teacher or mentor. Newly qualified teachers too, would be well advised to seek the support and advice of experienced colleagues before becoming involved in any case of suspected abuse. Where such a discussion is initiated, the main aim for the teacher is to try and encourage the child to talk and then to listen to what they have to say. Open-ended questions are the best way to proceed in order to get the truest picture possible and avoid prejudicing any possible future legal actions.

A worrying development

Paul was painting in the nursery. His teacher noticed that he had only used red and black paint and that the picture had a somewhat visceral quality to it. She told Paul that his painting was very interesting and asked him if he would like her to write anything under his picture for him. Paul thought for a moment and then said, 'The daddy hits the mummy with a pan, the mummy stabs the daddy.'

If such discussions between teacher and young child do take place, the teacher must note down the conversation, giving details of the date, time, place, any other people present and what the child said. This written evidence could form part of court proceedings at a future date and so it is important to be accurate. Once such a note has been compiled, the teacher must then forward the information to the member of staff with responsibility for dealing with suspected cases of abuse or neglect. This designated teacher will then take the process forward with other agencies and individuals such as Education Welfare Officers (EWOs), the local Social Services Department, and LEA child protection officers. If there is to be any investigation, it must be conducted by the proper authorities. Individual class teachers, and even designated teachers, are not trained in investigation techniques. Meddling of any kind is likely to cause more harm than good and could result in

- parents and carers being wrongly accused; or
- someone guilty of abuse escaping the consequences of their actions.

The primary role of the teacher therefore is to *be alert for the signs* and to *inform the proper authorities*.

TEACHING 3–8

Abuse by Staff in the Nursery/School

Physical contact is bound to take place continuously between staff and children in 3–8 settings. It is not only inevitable, it is also desirable for young children to know that they are valued and cared for by staff who are not cold, distant and aloof. However, when allegations of abuse are made against a member of staff, it is an extremely traumatic experience for the person accused, irrespective of their guilt or innocence. Early years teachers and teacher training students must take care at all times to ensure that the inevitable physical contact between themselves and their children is appropriate in nature, and could not be misconstrued as in any way abusive or indecent. Should staff encounter children who are clearly uneasy about physical contact, they would be well advised to avoid any potentially compromising situations, and may wish to place their concerns on record.

In a situation where a young child suggests that they have been the subject of abuse by a member of staff in the school or nursery, the teacher must initially follow the same procedure as that outlined on p. 143. The child must be listened to, and the conversation must be noted down. However, at this stage the allegation and the notes must be reported directly and immediately to the headteacher. Where the subject of the allegation is the headteacher, the teacher has a duty to inform the governors. In cases where allegations are made against members of staff, the headteacher and/or the governors are initially responsible for determining what action, if any, to take.

Possible action arising from allegations of abuse against staff

- The headteacher and governors may conclude that the allegation is sufficiently serious to warrant its forwarding to the child protection agencies.
- The headteacher and governors could decide that the allegation arose from a lack of judgement or a degree of *naïveté* on the part of the member of staff concerned, and that the matter would be better dealt with through normal internal procedures.
- The headteacher and governors could decide that the allegation is completely unfounded with no evidence to support it and consequently does not warrant either referral or internal disciplinary action.

Any teacher who is the subject of an allegation of abuse has the right to be informed that the allegation has been made and what action the headteacher and governing body propose to take as a result. The only exception to this rule occurs where an objection to disclosure is made by the child protection agencies such as the police. Teachers accused of abuse should seek advice from their union and are entitled to have a union representative present at any subsequent meeting to discuss and investigate the allegation.

Maintaining Good Order in the Classroom

By the end of this section you should

- have a working knowledge and understanding of teachers' responsibilities relating to discipline and control, including appropriate physical restraint of pupils (Section 4 of the Education Act 1997 and DfEE Circular 9/94) (Daii);
- understand the importance of setting a good example to children, through presentation and personal and professional conduct (Dc).

A Positive Approach

Schools and nurseries play an important role in helping pupils to grow into responsible adults. In part this is achieved through successfully inculcating in young children a set of values, and promoting what the Education Reform Act 1988 referred to as the 'spiritual, cultural, mental and physical development of pupils'. Such values include respect for one another, self-respect, honesty, trust, fairness and self-discipline. Everyone involved in the working of nurseries and schools has a part to play in promoting good behaviour and discipline, as without them, teaching and learning will be greatly impaired.

- The management in nurseries and schools (governing bodies and headteachers) will take the lead in drawing up the policy on behaviour.
- It is crucial, wherever possible, for schools to draw upon the backing of parents and other carers as they are the most influential people in the lives of young children. Parents are expected to lend their support to the efforts of the nursery/school to maintain good order.
- Individual teachers are especially important in translating the policy into reality through their efficiency and professionalism. Good behaviour and discipline are founded on good organization and a professional approach to the task of teaching. Teachers of 3–8 pupils must achieve a balanced approach which takes into consideration the nurture required by young children, while at the same time recognizing the importance of imparting positive social behaviour.

Many of the day-to-day actions of teachers are fundamental in underpinning their attempts to foster good behaviour and discipline amongst the children. The use of praise and recognition promotes consideration and responsibility on the part of the children as well as offering an intrinsic reward for good work and behaviour. In some cases, extrinsic rewards such as points, stars, or marbles in jars can be used as a positive incentive to promote effort and good behaviour (Wragg, 1993). Providing tasks that are well matched to the children's needs and abilities, in sessions and lessons which start and end on time and where interruptions and diversions are minimized or dealt with efficiently, also helps to create a positive learning atmosphere where praise and recognition are attainable by all pupils. At the same time, giving clear instructions, using language appropriate to young children, helps to avoid confusion and disruptive behaviour.

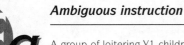

Ambiguous instruction

A group of loitering Y1 children were being ushered good naturedly from the classroom at lunchtime by their teacher who uttered the words 'Go on, hop it you lot.' So they did!

Finally, looking like, and acting the part of, a teacher is an important element in maintaing good order. This includes developing a *presence* in the classroom.

Establishing your presence as a teacher

- Show consistency in your expectations and actions.
- Radiate a sense of confidence by not hesitating or rushing your speech, by making eye contact, adopting appropriate body postures and tones of voice.
- Exhibit firm, though gentle, insistence when necessary.
- Avoid being overly and inappropriately friendly, especially in the early stages of the year or with older pupils.
- Establish a clear and simple set of rules or conventions within which the activities of the class will take place (see Chapter 2).

What to Do when it All Goes Wrong

Establishing clear conventions and setting a good example to the children will help to reduce the incidence of poor behaviour, but these and other strategies will not eliminate such conduct totally. All teachers experience instances where young children's behaviour will be deemed unacceptable and action of some sort will be required. Where necessary, schools and nurseries have the authority to impose punishment that is reasonable. As before, the term reasonable is open to interpretation. Teachers of young children have a number of options open to them when trying to deal with unwanted behaviour which include administering punishment, withdrawing pleasurable activities and ignoring unwanted behaviour (Robertson, 1989).

Strategies for dealing with unwanted behaviour

- **Administering unpleasantness** might involve the use of reprimands or, in more serious instances, the imposition of sanctions.
- **Withdrawing pleasurable activities** could include the removal of attention such as not listening to and encouraging tale-tellers, or the removal of activities. Teachers need to be careful about always picking games and practical creative activities, as this can carry hidden messages about what aspects of learning are enjoyable and what are not.
- **Ignoring unwanted behaviour** could include rewarding desirable behaviour and denying attention for unwanted behaviour. This can be effective, but it can also be a risky strategy if applied inappropriately. In some situations for example, other children may provide the desired attention and some actions by children such as racist or sexist abuse simply cannot be ignored. One possible refinement for teachers wishing to utilize

this technique is to distinguish between ignoring something completely and deciding against any verbal rebuke or punishment, restricting themselves instead to a slightly shocked look or a raised, and very disapproving, eyebrow.

Whatever strategy a teacher decides to employ in order to deal effectively with unwanted behaviour, there are some key features of good practice to bear in mind.

Ways to discipline effectively

- **Appropriateness** is crucial, particularly with very young children where you are engaged in the care and nurture of pupils as well as in their education. Performance and motivation can be damaged by too severe a punishment or reprimand.
- **Timing** is important. You should try to act before or during misbehaviour. Success in doing this is a powerful statement of your control and awareness. In addition, the immediacy of your actions is much more meaningful and relevant to young children, for whom an incident the day before can be ancient history.
- **Consistency** and **determination**. Every time a rule is broken without penalty makes it harder to enforce that rule in future. Inconsistency on your part will be regarded as unfair by the children and rightly so, and failure to be as good as your word may be seen as ineffectualness.
- **Simplicity** is essential. You should keep any rules or conventions simple unless you want to spend all your time explaining and enforcing them.
- **Fairness** matters. You should not victimize a whole class or nursery for the actions of one individual.
- **Respect** is everything. When you do have to reprimand or punish behaviour, focus on the act rather than the perpetrator. Personalizing matters and humiliating a young child does nothing for that child's self-image, it is degrading for them, constitutes a no-value statement on your part , and in some cases risks open rebellion on the part of the child concerned. Children are far more likely to respond positively to someone they respect and who obviously respects them.

Readers may wish to reflect on the example below and consider to what extent it represents an appropriate, well-timed response to unwanted behaviour.

A punishment fitting a crime?

A student teacher encountered a Y1 child sitting outside the headteacher's office at break time. She enquired as to why he was there. He replied that he was not allowed out to play for six months because he had been 'naughty in the playground'.

While reprimands and punishment play a small role in establishing good order in the classroom when compared to positive discipline and the principles of good classroom management and teaching, it is still a very important role. The examples below represent the more common sorts of behaviour which may require intervention on the part of the 3–8 teacher in order to maintain good order; they range from the very minor to the rather more serious.

Examples of unwanted behaviour in 3–8 year old children

How would you deal with these situations?

- During a class discussion two girls begin to plait one another's hair. In so doing they opt out of the activity and begin to distract other children who start to join in. An outbreak of hairdressing is about to occur.
- You're reading a story to the class. Matthew is next to you. When you next look Matthew has miraculously materialized in a completely different part of the room and is prodding another child.
- You have taken register, explained the morning's tasks and started the children off. It rapidly becomes apparent that chaos is ensuing about your person.
- There is a 'phantom whistler' somewhere in the room.
- Mrs Jones, the peripatetic piano player is with you in the hall for singing and dancing. Paul and Wayne are pulling faces and objecting loudly at the prospect of having to dance with the girls.
- While moving around the classroom you overhear one individual make a racist remark directly to another child.
- A child comes to you after playtime and claims to have been struck by a child in another class.
- A parent tells you that their child is being bullied at school by a classmate.
- Your class is travelling to the local woods on the bus. Two burly gentlemen, one sporting a rather striking mohican haircut, board the bus and come upstairs to where the children are sitting. Unable to contain herself, and broadcasting on full volume, one of the children shouts out 'Miss! Look at the state of his hair!'
- John and Ali are marched into your classroom at lunchtime by an incandescent lunchtime supervisor after having suggested that she try something anatomically impossible.
- A worried parent approaches you before registration and tells you that an older child has been demanding, and obtaining, part of her child's packed lunch.
- A child approaches you in the playground and tells you that David has been showing his willie to the girls.
- There is a squabble over the Lego. One child hits another. You reproach both children and encourage them to work together without quarrelling. As soon as your back is turned the 'hitter' strikes again.
- Your class is discussing their activities over the weekend with you on Monday morning. Sarah puts her hand up and when asked, tells the class that she has seen a film called 'George' at the weekend and it was really good. When you ask her to tell the class about the film she says that it was all about a huge fish called a shark that went around eating people. The other children start to laugh and catcall.
- The headteacher is reading to the school in assembly. It is a part of the story that is full of dramatic pauses and hushed tones, generating quiet excitement and expectation on the part of the children. Suddenly there is a noise in the midst of your class followed by much sniggering, theatrical wafting of hands and clutching of throats.

The Use of Force by a Teacher

In extreme circumstances it may be necessary for a teacher to physically restrain a pupil in order to preserve good order in the classroom or to protect everyone's health and safety. It is hard to imagine a situation in most 3–8 settings where considerable force would need to be employed. However all trainee and newly qualified teachers need to be familiar with the legislation and guidance.

The 1997 Education Act (Section 4) sets out the circumstances when the use of force may be appropriate to prevent a child from

- committing a criminal offence (or in the case of very young children behaving in a way that would be criminal if they were above the age of criminal responsibility);
- injuring themselves or others;
- causing damage to property; or
- behaving in such a way as to undermine good order and discipline in the school/nursery.

In such situations, a teacher may use reasonable force. Once again, the term reasonable is open to interpretation and requires teachers to exercise their professional judgement. In making this judgement about whether or not to use force and how much force to use, teachers must weigh up what they think the circumstances warrant. Clearly, this judgement will be heavily influenced by the very young age of 3–8 children. In an effort to clarify for teachers what sorts of incidents might justify the use of reasonable force, the DfEE published Circular 10/98 which sought to provide additional guidance for schools. This guidance stated clearly that any individual has the right to defend themselves against an attack, providing they do not use a 'disproportionate degree of force to do so'. The circular also made it quite clear that any teacher is entitled to intervene where pupils are risking their own or others' safety. Circular 10/98 divides the types of incident where force might be necessary into three categories.

Categories
1. Where action is necessary in self-defence or because there is an imminent risk of injury;
2. Where there is a developing risk of injury, or significant damage to property;
3. Where a pupil is behaving in a way that is compromising good order and discipline.

(DfEE, 1998b)

Examples to illustrate the categories of incident outlined above include

- attacks by pupils on members of staff;
- attacks by pupils on other pupils;
- fights between pupils;
- pupils who are deliberately damaging or vandalising property (or are about to);
- pupils causing or risking accidents through rough play or misuse of equipment and materials;
- pupils running through school in such a way as to risk injury to themselves or others;
- pupils who leave or try to leave the school premises where those pupils could be *at risk* if not kept in the school;
- pupils persistently refusing to obey an order to leave the classroom; and
- pupils behaving in a way that seriously disrupts a lesson.   (DfEE, 1998b)

Having tried to clarify what circumstances might warrant force being used, Circular 10/98 then attempts to assist teachers in interpreting the concept of reasonable, which it acknowledges will always ultimately depend upon all the circumstances of a case.

- Teachers **can**
    physically block a pupil or get between pupils;
    hold or restrain a pupil; and
    lead pupils away.

- Teachers **cannot**
    use neck holds of any description;
    punch, kick, or slap a pupil;
    twist limbs and/or joints;
    trip pupils up;
    pull hair or ears; or
    hold pupils face down.

Trainee and newly qualified teachers need to be aware that any use of force is illegal if the circumstances do not warrant it, for example, using force to prevent very minor incidents. They also need to maintain a sense of proportion as to the amount of force to be used; the guidance calls for the 'minimum needed to achieve the desired result' and for teachers to take into account factors such as age, understanding and sex of pupils. Circular 9/94 contains guidance on dealing with children with emotional and behavioural difficulties who may be particularly volatile and whose behaviour can be particularly extreme. However, as with all other pupils, teachers are expected to adopt an essentially constructive and positive approach and to work hard to promote the self-image of such children. Here too the application of force should be the last resort, not the norm.

In a situation where a teacher has concluded that force may be necessary, the teacher must tell the pupil concerned to desist from whatever it is they are doing and make clear what will happen if they do not. When force is used it should be *as well as* communication, not *instead of*. Teachers need to stay as calm as possible and inform the child that restraint or force will cease to be used once the behaviour that caused it has also ceased. In those rare instances (for nursery and primary teachers) where the pupil is particularly large or in other ways is capable of injuring the teacher, then that teacher should clear other pupils from the immediate area to remove them from risk and call or send for assistance. While waiting for this to arrive the teacher should continue to try to resolve the situation verbally, or at least to stop it from escalating. Trainee and newly qualified teachers especially should not be afraid to seek and accept help from more experienced colleagues. It is not a sign of weakness, it is a sign of good sense.

A no-fuss, effective procedure

A student teacher was making a preliminary visit to her teaching practice school. The school contained a number of children who were capable of becoming extremely disruptive, and in some cases violent, during lessons. The deputy headteacher introduced her to the school's procedures for dealing with these difficult situations when they occurred. The procedures included a card system which all staff used. In the event of disruption or violence in the classroom, the teacher concerned could send a responsible child to the deputy's room with a card. A yellow card meant 'Please come to my classroom when you have a few minutes as I need some assistance'. A red card meant 'I need your assistance immediately'.

In addition to situations where teachers have to use force to deal with aggressive behaviour, there are other situations where, due to a lack of maturity on the part of pupils, teachers have to react instantly and use force in order to avoid harm befalling either a child or other people. This can be particularly true for those working with younger children. On these occasions there may be no time to explain or issue a warning, and action must be immediate; for example, a reception teacher on an out-of-school visit when one of the children suddenly jumps into the road and has to be pulled back quickly; or when a young child is about to throw a heavy object at another child in the class without thinking about the likely consequences of their actions. In all cases, the use of force should be the last resort and only be used to protect children and others, not to punish.

Don't dither

A class of Y1 children were taken on a local walk by their teacher as part of a topic on 'Our School'. The school was situated near a block of flats and the group went up a few floors to give the children a bird's-eye view of their school and its surroundings. Suddenly the teacher noticed one of the children holding a large glass marble over the parapet with the apparent intention of dropping it. She immediately dived forward, grabbed the child's hand, drew him away from the parapet, took the marble away from him and spoke firmly to him about how dangerous such an act could be for passers-by.

The use of force always carries with it the possibility of complaints, and teachers need to act professionally at all times. Where a serious incident has occurred in which a teacher has had to use force of some description, this should be reported verbally and in writing to the headteacher. The written report should include details of date, time, names, the nature of the incident, a rationale for the use of force in the circumstances, the pupil's response and any information on injury or damage suffered.

Continuing Professional Development

AUDIT

By the end of this section you should

- be aware of, and know how to access, recent inspection evidence and classroom-relevant research on teaching primary pupils (A2dv);

- understand the need to take responsibility for your own professional development and to keep up-to-date with research and developments in pedagogy and in the subjects you teach (De).

153

High quality teaching and learning can be supported and enhanced by many factors but trainee and newly qualified 3–8 teachers would do well to pay close attention to the need to engage in, and draw upon whole-school approaches and to conduct themselves as thoughtful and reflective professionals.

Fostering High Standards of Teaching and Learning

Continuing professional development relies on a combination of reflective and self-critical practice in alliance with reference to research and inspection evidence which can inform and improve that practice.

Without continuous self-evaluation there can be no progress that is not accidental or very slow. Reflective teachers evaluate in order to progress more rapidly and in those directions where progression is most needed. To manage learning in the classroom in increasingly effective ways means teachers must identify their achievements and build on them, while simultaneously identifying any gaps and plugging them. It is a continuous process throughout a teacher's career as achievements and gaps change over time. Clearly this longer-term evaluation will be based at least in part on everyday observations and evaluations (see Chapter 2). However, it is also necessary to move beyond the specific to consider the larger picture. Trainees and newly qualified teachers may wish to use similar headings to structure their longer-term evaluation but ought to avoid wasting time by regurgitating chunks of lesson evaluations. They should concentrate instead on the wider picture and make an accurate appraisal of their performance and issues relating to their future practice.

In addition to a reflective and analytical approach to the task of teaching, trainee and newly qualified teachers can also inform and improve their practice by accessing sources of information on recent educational research, and new guidance on practice and ideas for work with children. Professional journals, magazines and government agencies are all useful sources.

Examples of useful early years periodicals

- *Childhood Education*
- *Early Childhood Research Quarterly*
- *Nursery World*

Many publications arising from the work of government departments and agencies can be located on the Internet. These often contain recent press releases, information on circulars and lists of publications. Such sites can be helpful for trainee and newly qualified teachers wishing to keep up-to-date with the latest developments in the 3–8 curriculum. Furthermore, both nurseries and primary schools in England and Wales are subject to inspection by teams from the Office for Standards in Education (OFSTED). Copies of inspection reports are widely available and can also be accessed on the Internet. Such reports can be a useful source of information for trainee and newly qualified teachers wishing to keep up-to-date with what constitutes quality teaching and learning in the 3–8 age range.

Useful web addresses for inspection evidence and current research and publications on 3–8 education

- Office for Standards in Education (OFSTED): www.ofsted.gov.uk
- Department for Education and Employment (DfEE): www.dfee.gov.uk
- Qualifications and Curriculum Authority (QCA): www.qca.org.uk
- Teacher Training Agency (TTA): www.teach-tta.gov.uk
- National Grid for Learning (NGFL): www.ngfl.gov.uk

Induction Arrangements

Self-evaluation is not merely important during initial teacher training but ought to inform future practice once in post. Teacher appraisal and arrangements for the induction of newly qualified teachers will ensure that the ability to evaluate one's own practice effectively will continue to be an important skill throughout a teacher's career. Such evaluation may focus on short-term issues arising from particular sessions; it may also involve reflection over a longer period of time and focus upon a wider set of professional competences or understandings.

Once appointed, newly qualified teachers will have an induction programme that will last for three terms. NQTs on short-term or part-time contracts will spend an equivalent period being inducted, for example an NQT on a 0.5 contract will have an induction period lasting six terms. Headteachers will have overall responsibility for ensuring that NQTs are properly inducted and will appoint an induction tutor whose role it will be to act as mentor during the induction period. Headteachers may decide to take this role themselves.

Newly qualified teachers will have a reduced teaching load in order to facilitate their induction and some of this time can also be used to observe experienced colleagues in action either in their own school or in another school where effective practice is taking place. The Induction Standards follow on from the Standards for Initial Teacher Training and target the following areas:

Planning, teaching and class management

- Setting clear targets for learning and monitoring pupil progress
- Planning effectively
- Ensuring good standards of behaviour
- Meeting the needs of SEN pupils
- Ensuring equality of opportunity irrespective of sex, race or ability

Monitoring, Assessment, Recording, Reporting and Accountability

- Making accurate assessments of pupil achievements
- Liaising effectively with parents and providing informative reports on pupil progress

Other Professional Requirements

- Making effective use of staff and other adults in the classroom
- Implementing nursery/school policies and practices
- Taking responsibility for your own continuing professional development

During induction, NQTs will be monitored, supported and assessed by their induction mentor and/or headteacher. Lesson observations will be conducted on a half-termly basis and will focus upon a particular aspect of the NQTs' teaching. Such observations will be accompanied by follow-up discussions during which time the NQTs and their mentors can analyse the lesson. In addition, NQTs will be expected to take part in professional reviews of progress in which future targets will be negotiated and set. Summative assessment meetings will take place towards the end of each term.

Agenda for summative meetings

- **End of first term**: the extent to which the NQT is consistently meeting the Standards for the Award of QTS. . . and is beginning to meet the Induction Standards.
- **End of second term**: the NQT's progress towards meeting the Induction Standards.
- **End of third term**: determining whether the NQT has met all the requirements for the satisfactory completion of the induction period.

Whole-school Approaches

By the end of this section you should

- know about your professional responsibilities in relation to school policies and practices, including those concerned with pastoral and personal safety matters, including bullying (Df).

156

Teachers of 3–8 pupils are required to play their part in drawing up, and adhering to, whole-school documentation on a range of matters such as Desirable Outcomes/Early Learning Goals, core and foundation subjects in the National Curriculum, and cross-curricular issues such as bullying, special educational needs, health and safety, behaviour, and transition to, from and between schools. Such documentation will be composed of policy statements and guidelines, and in the case of National Curriculum subjects and Desirable Outcomes/Early Learning Goals will also include schemes of work (see Chapter 2).

Policies

A policy is a succinct description, outlining the nursery's/school's overall rationale for teaching a subject or tackling an educational issue. It should be to the point and written in plain English. A policy consists of broad principles which underpin the way in which a subject or issue is approached in a nursery/school. In effect it answers the questions, *What is it?* and *Why do we do/teach it?*

1. Policy statement on bullying

. . . . School believes that it is against the interests of all children, the bullied and the bullies, to allow bullying to take place unchallenged. No child can learn properly and achieve their full potential when they feel threatened and vulnerable. We regard bullying as particularly serious and the school will always take firm action against it. In addition, our school believes that we do a long term disservice to a pupil if we allow them to continue to bully others and avoid facing up to the consequences of their actions.

2. Policy statement on subject area (English)

English is the basic language of communication in this country and throughout much of the world. The mastery of this subject is an essential prerequisite for educational progress in all other curriculum areas and is vital for pupils' adult lives as citizens in our society. Through the teaching of English at . . . . School pupils will build on the language opportunities provided in the home and will develop into more proficient and discriminating readers, writers, speakers and listeners. Consequently our pupils will be introduced to a wide range of texts, materials and information technology resources to enrich and challenge their learning; be given opportunities to develop their competence in standard written English; and be made aware of the differences between spoken and written forms of language.

Guidelines

Guidelines set out how the nursery/school expects staff to approach a subject or issue with their pupils and they are frequently attached to the policy statements. Guidelines provide a general framework and deal with a range of issues including organization and management, cross-curricular links, and assessment. Possible headings for guidelines will vary depending on whether the guidelines in question relate to a National Curriculum subject (e.g. Mathematics), Desirable Outcomes/ Early Learning Goals (e.g. Creative Development) or a generic issue cutting across the whole curriculum (e.g. bullying). A list of areas that might be included in guidelines is given below.

Possible guideline headings

1. Links to the Desirable Outcomes/Early Learning Goals or National Curriculum Programmes of Study and Attainment Targets. Links with other subjects.
2. How the subject or issue is planned for in the nursery/school.
3. Classroom organization, management and teaching methods.
4. Marking, assessment and recording.
5. Continuity and progression across the nursery/school.
6. Equal opportunities and multicultural and anti-racist strategies.
7. Provision for SEN.
8. Use and provision of ICT and other resources.
9. Health and safety.
10. Links with the cross-curricular elements.
11. Links with the wider community.
12. The role of the headteacher.
13. The role of the coordinator.
14. The role of parents and other adults.

Guidelines on bullying

1. Identifying incidents of bullying
Staff need to be aware that there can be a fine line between bullying and boisterous or bossy behaviour. A child being bossy will try to dominate whoever is around at the time and will often grow out of this behaviour as they mature and develop wider social skills. A bully will *target* younger/weaker children and will display a conscious desire to hurt or frighten these children. A boisterous pupil displays a high-spirited, uncontrolled and not unfriendly presence in the classroom. A bully will *deliberately* set out to spoil other children's activities, displaying hostile, rough and intimidating behaviour.

Bullying can take many forms. It can be physical, emotional or verbal in nature and can involve a single bully or a group of pupils. Possible examples of bullying include

- name calling, malicious gossip and taunting;
- stealing or damaging other children's property and work;
- coercion, threats, extortion and intimidation;
- punching, kicking and other violent behaviour; and
- ostracizing children.

Signs of distress that might indicate that bullying is taking place include

- pupils acting in a withdrawn manner and appearing isolated;
- deterioration in standards of work;
- fake illnesses and a deterioration in attendance and punctuality;
- desire to remain close to adults; and
- apparent unhappiness, anxiety and fear.

2. Reasons for bullying

Bullying can occur in children of all ages and there are a variety of reasons why some pupils become victims of bullying and some pupils become bullies. In some cases the bullies themselves are the victims of bullying. The children targeted are often (although not always) timid, anxious or less assertive, in other words those children deemed unlikely to fight back or resist the bullying, the children who are younger or smaller than the bully, or the children who are loners and not part of a particular group.

Reasons why children are targeted are:

- differences in race, sex, or social class;
- other differences, including physical disability, general appearance or being new to the school;
- differences in ability, including academic, physical and creative;
- vulnerability, perhaps as a result of suffering other problems.

Reasons why children become bullies are:

- they are themselves victims of bullying or violence;
- they obtain a sense of power and control through the act of bullying;
- they are copying the behaviour of others (either in school, at home or on television and in films and videos);
- they are jealous; or
- they are insecure and have low self-esteem.

3. Strategies for eliminating bullying in the classroom

- Use lots of praise and recognition to reward cooperative, non-aggressive behaviour.
- Encourage the caring side of pupils' development.
- Discuss and promote friendships and cooperation.
- Maintain proper supervision both in the classroom and outside.
- Make children aware that standing by while bullying takes place is to support the bullying.
- Give support to the victim and help them to regain and develop their self-esteem and confidence.
- Try to find out why the bully is bullying. Don't bully the bully. Help the child to see another's point of view, 'How would you feel if . . .?'
- Give support to the bully by encouraging and supporting them to work positively with other children; for example, giving responsibility for looking after someone or something.
- Work to involve parents. Explain why certain actions have been taken and discuss with parents what they can do to reinforce and support the efforts of the nursery/school to resolve the problem successfully. If necessary, help parents to understand the

distinction between bossy or boisterous behaviour and bullying. However, make sure that parents know that you take their concerns seriously, are aware of the situation and will take steps to stop their child being made to feel unhappy.

- Serious or persistent incidents should be monitored, recorded and reported to the headteacher or the responsible member of staff.
- In very serious cases bullying needs to be reported to the governing body and if necessary will involve an official complaints procedure.

159

Schemes

A scheme of work constitutes long-term planning (see Chapter 2) and gives details about what is taught, where and when across the school or nursery. It provides for the sequence of teaching throughout the nursery/school in order to ensure progression and continuity while avoiding repetition. Schemes are based on relevant national dcumentation such as the Desirable Outcomes/Early Learning Goals, National Curriculum Programmes of Study, and National Literacy and Numeracy Strategies. More specific, medium-term planning for individual classes or year groups is based upon this framework. It is worth noting that with the increasing emphasis on literacy and numeracy, including the introduction of literacy and numeracy hours, many schools are using commercially-produced schemes such as those produced by the QCA/ DfEE to help them deliver the wider curriculum.

Whole-school Approaches to Whole-school Issues

In addition to producing documentation on curriculum areas, schools and nurseries also produce guidance on matters that cut across the whole curriculum, and to which all staff are expected to adhere (see Guidelines on bullying on p. 157). Two of these whole-school issues which may affect trainee and newly qualified 3–8 teachers are

- transition between classes and schools; and
- homework.

Transition

There are a number of significant transition events for pupils between the ages of 3 and 8, as well as the lesser ones that often occur at the start of a year when many children move to new classes in the same school. Frequently, the transition involves not only a change of culture, but also a change of location.

Transition events

- From home to nursery/reception
- From nursery to reception
- From reception to Key Stage 1
- From Key Stage 1 to Key Stage 2
- From one class/teacher to another class/teacher

Such transitions have the potential to make young children feel very insecure and nervous. If they are not well-managed and planned for, the resulting feelings of vulnerability can adversely affect their achievement and well-being. Children's ability to make a successful transition from home to nursery, or from nursery to school (becoming happy and successful learners in the process) can have a profound and positive impact on their future development and achievements. As a result, nurseries and schools produce guidance for staff, the aim of which is to make children's transitions as smooth as possible. Parents are often referred to in such documentation as key players in supporting the children during these periods. For many 3- to 5-year-old children it can be a particularly stressful time. For some it will be their first experience away from their home and parents, and the anxiety can affect parents and carers as well as the children. Nursery and school transition policies therefore seek to offer advice to staff on ways of easing the concerns and anxieties that families may have about transition. The priority for all teachers, whatever the transition, is to help the children to become secure and confident in their new environment as soon as possible, and to establish positive and productive relationships with both pupils and parents.

Helping children and parents to cope with transition events

- Talk to parents before and during the transition period. If parents are reassured they can communicate that reassurance to their children. They can also offer valuable information that you can use to help make children feel more secure.
- Talk to the children's current teacher prior to receiving a new group. They can offer good advice on likes and dislikes, and can help you to identify those children most likely to be adversely affected.
- Try to visit your new class in their present setting. What sort of environment are they used to? What sort of conventions and routines are they used to? Can you use similar conventions and routines to minimize their sense of disruption?
- Offer to swap places with your new class's current teacher, so that the children can get used to seeing you as their teacher.
- Help your pupils who are moving onto their next class by producing mini-portfolios of work that they can give to their new teacher.
- Make sure you speak positively about the new setting or class that your children will be going to. Do not reinforce or magnify their concerns and worries.
- Where children are moving schools rather than classes, involve older children in the induction process (provide 'buddies' in the playground).

Homework

Homework refers to any work which children are asked to do outside lesson time, either on their own or with parents and carers. Children will not normally encounter homework tasks prior to Key Stage 1. Homework tasks can offer schools a way of

- developing further their partnership arrangements with parents and carers by involving them actively in their children's learning;
- supporting individual children's consolidation, reinforcement and understanding of literacy and numeracy skills;
- extending school learning through additional reading; and
- providing opportunities for young children to talk about what they are learning to an interested adult, and to practise key skills in a supportive environment.

Examples of homework tasks at Key Stage 1

- Playing simple word/number games
- Learning spellings (once a week)
- Learning number facts (once a week)
- Reading together (daily). All children should either read to their parents/carers or be read to. Fluent readers need to read on their own for at least ten minutes each day.

Both parents and teachers have a part to play in making homework policies an effective device for raising standards of achievement. It is the job of the teacher and the school to plan and resource homework activities. Children with special educational needs can also be included in homework. They may benefit from special tasks separate from those given to their peers; however, it is also important that they do as much in common with other children as possible. Projects for SEN pupils will need to have a very clear focus and be varied, not purely written assignments. Children at Stage 2 of the SEN Code of Practice will have tasks which are specifically linked to their IEP targets. The role of parents and carers meanwhile is equally crucial. Regular dialogue can and should take place between teachers and parents (for example, through reading record diaries). Teachers can use comments made by parents on a weekly basis as a means of informing their own assessments. In addition, the attitudes of parents will have a significant impact on the efforts and achievements of the children. Schools need to liaise with parents to ensure that they realize just what a pivotal role they play in

- ensuring that the child has a reasonably peaceful place in which they can do their homework with support;
- making it clear to the child that time spent completing homework is valuable and worthwhile time spent together; and
- encouraging and giving lots of praise to the child when they are completing their homework.

Working with Parents

By the end of this section you should

- know about effective ways of working with parents and other carers (A3b);
- know that learning takes place inside and outside the school context, and understand the need to liaise effectively with parents and other carers (Dg).

A successful partnership with parents is often cited as a vital prerequisite for successful education of young children. However, it is important for teachers to be familiar with the rationale behind this partnership. Why should parents be involved and what are some of the obstacles to effective partnership?

Understanding Partnership with Parents

Parents are no more homogeneous than the diverse society from which they and their children's teachers come. What works well in one place, for one set of parents, may not be so effective in a different context. That said, one feature that unites the overwhelming majority of parents is the desire for their children to be happy and successful. Educators of young children are continuing a learning process that has been begun by parents; consequently parents should be valued as active partners in their child's continuing learning.

Effective partnership between parents and teachers can help parents to exert a positive influence on their child's progress through their attitudes and the support they give, thus producing a range of gains such as motivation, good behaviour and positive relations. These outcomes may help to avoid conflict between the home and the nursery/school, and minimize confusion for the children in the process. Effective liaison is also beneficial for parents and teachers in that parents can become much more knowledgeable about young children's learning, for example, being persuaded of the value of structured play in learning, or undertaking activities with their children that will help to prepare them for entry into nursery/school. Parents may well seek out teachers for advice and to air their concerns about their children.

Ways in which parents can help to support their children's education

- Spending time with and showing an interest in the child
- Listening
- Talking and asking questions
- Exploring feelings and ideas
- Reading
- Encouraging the child to try new things and solve simple problems
- Playing with the child

Although effective partnership between nurseries/schools and parents has much to recommend it, it is by no means unproblematic either to initiate or to maintain such relationships. While there is certainly much common ground between teachers and parents, there are also some key differences, not least the fact that while a parent's starting point is their own child, the teacher has to consider all the children. There can also be differences in terms of beliefs, with some activities valued by teachers but not valued or appreciated by some parents, for example promoting anti-racist policies in an area characterized by endemic racism, or promoting non-violent approaches to resolving disagreements and conflicts.

Understandable but unhelpful parental input

'I've told our John that if anyone hits him, he's got to hit them back.'

A parental taboo

Daniel's parents asked to see the teacher in charge of nursery, Mrs Cooper. They explained that they were very worried about Daniel's preference for spending large amounts of time in the structured play area wearing dresses, high heeled shoes and carrying a handbag. Daniel's father, in particular, wanted Mrs Cooper to take steps to steer Daniel into activities more *normal* for a boy.

An impossible request

Philip's father accompanied him to school on the day that he started in Year 2. He explained to Philip's teacher that Philip had not always been well behaved in his Year 1 class and that he wanted the school to know that he was in complete support of their efforts to get Philip to improve his behaviour. He told Philip's teacher that she had his permission to give Philip a 'good hiding' if he misbehaved. Philip's teacher explained that such an act would be illegal and would run counter to the school's policy of promoting responsibility and self-discipline among the children. 'I see,' replied Philip's father. 'Well, in that case, if he messes you about, tell me and *I'll* give him a good hiding.'

It is important for 3–8 teachers to keep the powerful arguments in favour of effective home/school links clearly in mind given some of the impediments to cooperation.

Factors that can undermine partnership with parents

- Lack of previous experience on the part of some teachers, who may feel threatened at having their work exposed to public scrutiny
- Lack of staff and time to plan and implement partnership activities
- Lack of training for teachers in working and liaising with parents
- Lack of will on the part of some parents to be involved in partnership with the nursery/school
- Lack of opportunity on the part of some parents who may be unable to liaise closely with the nursery/school due to other commitments, for example those in full-time employment.

Strategies for Promoting Parental Involvement

Real partnership requires real dialogue

A newly qualified teacher, keen to encourage parents into the classroom, invited a parent to visit the class. When the parent arrived the NQT asked her to supervise a group of six reception children doing a baking activity in an adjacent utility room. The activity was intended to give the children experience of exploring and handling equipment and materials, and talking about how materials change when mixed and/or heated. When the NQT went into the utility room a little later to check on how the activity was proceeding she found that the children had had almost no hands-on experience with the tools and materials and all the discussion was purely procedural in nature. It became clear to the NQT that the parent was primarily concerned with the end-product and that she would have to make a point in future of explaining and communicating the purposes of tasks properly instead of using parents as little more than a spare pair of hands.

Home and school are the two most important factors in a young child's life. Families contain relationships that are not replicated anywhere else while nurseries and schools offer them an introduction to group life where they can acquire new social skills. Although the roles of nursery/school and home are somewhat different, their aspirations for the children are similar. This similarity in aspiration means that communication and sharing information are vital in promoting positive parental involvement and can take place in a number of ways.

Informal communication

- **Regular parent – teacher contact** gives considerable insight into home circumstances, needs and problems. Parents can give teachers useful information on topics ranging from local problems to children's learning when they arrive at the start or end of the day. They need to be made to feel welcome. Parents who are knowledgeable and have a positive attitude towards the nursery/school can be highly effective in promoting that nursery/school in the rest of the community. Consequently, it is important to deal promptly and effectively with everyday queries on such things as transition to new classes and teachers, seating arrangements, or lunchtime problems.

- **Joint teaching**. Inviting parents into nursery/school to work with the children offers opportunities for shared classroom experiences. Teachers need to be professional and to adopt a partnership approach which includes explaining to, taking advice from, and working cooperatively with parents. Although this is a time-consuming approach, it is more likely to make parents feel valued than an approach where they are in the classroom but engaged only superficially on the margins.
- **Home visits** can be an effective, albeit resource intensive, approach to sharing information and establishing close links between parents and the nursery/school. Such visits help to ensure that parents, carers and children are properly inducted into the life of the nursery/school, for example in terms of understanding the ethos and approach to good behaviour and discipline. They also help teachers to acquire an understanding of the children's linguistic or cultural background. Home visits may provide a less threatening forum in which 3–8 teachers can discuss ways of preparing children for entry into nursery/school and ways of supporting their continued progress once they have made the transition.
- **Other less formal opportunities** for parental involvement in the work of the nursery/school include fund raising events such as jumble sales and summer fairs, and invitations to assemblies and concerts. Teachers do need to remember, however, that parents have many commitments and should be sensitive to the dangers of overloading parents or overestimating the level of financial support available.

Formal communication

This may occur during events at which both parents and staff are present or it could be in writing. Written communication can take a number of forms. It is tangible evidence of a nursery's/school's ethos and actions.
- **School handbooks** should be attractive to encourage parents to look at them; including examples of children's work is one way of doing this. At the same time, the content should be clear, brief, easy to find, and the booklet should not be overly large as this can be off-putting, as indeed can inappropriate text that is too dense or badly spaced. When parents' first language is not English, text in alternative languages could also be used.
- **Letters, notices** and **circulars**. Children should be encouraged to remember to give letters and notices to their parents. Putting their names on them helps, so too does following up and checking that delivery has actually taken place. This can be particularly important with the youngest children who may have more important things on their minds than letters. It is important to remember to include return slips where answers are needed, and to keep copies for future reference.
- **Formal events** such as parents' evenings, open evenings, talks and curriculum events are useful venues at which parents and staff can share information and concerns. They can enhance parents' perceptions of how and what their children learn in nursery/school. It is important to adopt a professional approach to these occasions. The timing needs to be sensitive to the constraints many parents find themselves under, such as going out to work and caring for other children. Furthermore, the numbers invited ought not to preclude meaningful dialogue with staff, and the atmosphere should be conducive to positive and productive communication. Providing refreshments and things for parents to look at or do while they are waiting, helps to make parents feel less awkward.

Managing Schools and Nurseries

By the end of this section you should

- know about the structure and function of governing bodies, including their role during OFSTED inspections (Dh).

Governing Bodies

The governing body has responsibility for the overall management and conduct of a nursery/school. The governors are not concerned directly with the day-to-day running (this is the responsibility of the headteacher); they deal with more strategic issues. The exact nature of the governors' responsibilities will vary depending upon whether the nursery or school has county, special or voluntary aided status, and the details of the governing body's duties and powers will be set out in the nursery/school Articles of Government. Most governing bodies will have a role to play in strategic decisions involving the work of the nursery school, some of which are listed below.

Issues of School Governance

- Parents
- Links with the community
- The curriculum
- Resourcing and finance
- Staffing
- Development planning
- Premises
- Child welfare and discipline
- Admissions
- Extra-curricular activities.

The exact size of the governing body will be determined by the size of the nursery or school. Trainee and newly qualified teachers can obtain up-to-date information on the New Framework Governing Bodies by reading Circular 15/98 (DfEE, 1998c) which can be accessed through the Internet (www.dfee.gov.uk). Those elected and appointed to be school/nursery governors will represent a range of interests.

Governing bodies

- Some governors will be parent governors, elected by a vote of all parents with a child at the nursery/school, and they too must have a child in the school/nursery to be eligible to stand.
- Teacher governors are elected by the staff in the school and report back to their colleagues on the discussions and actions of the governing body. Schools and nurseries are required to ensure that non-teaching staff are also represented.
- Appointed governors are chosen by the LEA, and any other bodies with authority to appoint, such as the church in the case of voluntary aided schools.
- Coopted governors are coopted by other governors from a wide variety of backgrounds, the aim being to broaden and strengthen the expertise of the governing body. At least one member of the governing body should be a member of the local business community.
- The headteacher can opt to be a governor or not as they see fit. Whatever decision they make, they are entitled to attend all governors' meetings.

Note: For a complete breakdown of types of governors see Circular 15/98 Annex B.

Each year the governing body must elect a Chair and Vice-Chair to lead meetings and oversee the business of the governing body. Neither the Chair nor the Vice-Chair can be employed by the school or nursery. In addition, the governing body employs a clerk. The clerk's tasks include arranging meetings, circulating agendas and papers, and taking minutes. Normally, papers will be circulated to members of the governing body prior to meetings to enable discussion to be chaired more efficiently. Due to the extensive nature of the governors' responsibilities, most nurseries and schools set up a number of sub-committees in order to delegate decisions and preparatory work.

Examples of sub-committees

- Finance
- Premises
- Recruitment and staffing
- Curriculum

Once a term, the headteacher must make a report to the governing body. This report is a way of keeping governors up to date with events in the nursery/school, and places issues before the governors for advice or decision. Curriculum coordinators may be asked to report back to governors on developments in their area of responsibility, particularly when the coordinator is involved in meeting targets set out in a development plan or identified as needing attention by an OFSTED inspection team. The governors themselves have a duty to keep all parents informed about their actions and the work of the nursery/school. This is done formally through an annual report supported by an annual parents' meeting at which parents can discuss the report and any matters arising from it with members of the governing body. Parent governors and the headteacher are also likely to be approached on a more informal basis whenever an issue of concern to parents arises.

Inspection

It is a governing body's responsibility to ensure that nurseries and schools are prepared for inspection by teams from the Office for Standards in Education (OFSTED) and that they respond to the findings of these teams. The inspection teams, led by a registered inspector (RI), visit nurseries and schools to *inspect standards*, not to offer advice and support. Not surprisingly, schools and nurseries have no right to choose their own inspection team, although they can request the CVs of team members. In addition to the registered inspector, each team should contain one lay person and 'a range of specialisms appropriate to the task'.

Pre-inspection

During the pre-inspection period schools and nurseries are sent details of what the inspection team will look at. Before arriving, the inspection team will require copies of all the documentation pertaining to the running of the nursery/school which could include

- school/nursery development plans;
- schemes of work;
- curriculum policy documents;
- records;
- details of Inset for staff during previous three years;
- school prospectus;
- programme of staff meetings; and
- financial details.

Inspection teams also require timetables. Their aim is to see every teacher teaching as broad a range of subjects/areas as possible during the course of the inspection.

Prior to an inspection a questionnaire is sent to all parents by the governors to elicit comments and responses concerning their child's education. The responses are mailed directly back to the inspectors. Once the questionnaires have been sent out, it is then the responsibility of the governors to organize a parents' evening at which the RI will explain the purposes and nature of the inspection and discuss parental views and reactions in the light of the questionnaire responses. No governor or member of staff (including the headteacher) may attend this meeting unless they have a child in the school.

Inspection

The inspection itself will focus upon

- the quality of teaching and learning in the nursery/school;
- the standards of achievement;
- the efficiency of school management; and
- the development of pupils.

Class teachers are not the only staff to be inspected. The headteacher, deputy headteacher, members of the governing body, the nursery team leader and curriculum coordinators may all be interviewed about their roles. While in school/nursery, inspectors will observe teaching, talk to children and make comments on an observation schedule. Inspectors would normally be expected to spend a minimum of 15–20 minutes observing any lesson and to be present at the start of the session. Teachers need to have their plans and records available. Inspectors award ratings based on their observations during the sessions. The ratings system has changed since its original inception and could change again in the future. However, during 1998–99 a score of 1 denoted excellence, a score in the middle of the range denoted satisfactory teaching and learning, while a score of 6 or 7 denoted a poor performance or indeed incompetence. It is worth noting that in the context of an inspection the term *satisfactory* indicates competence; it should not be imbued with any of the connotations normally associated with everyday usage of the term.

In addition to classroom observations the inspection team will also look at SATs results (where appropriate) and examine teacher assessments and samples of work that reflect the ability range in classes. This work is examined in order to make judgements concerning continuity, progression and coverage of the Desirable Outcomes/Early Learning Goals and the National Curriculum.

Towards the end of the inspection the RI plus members of the team will talk to the headteacher and deputy headteacher and give a verbal report on their main findings; they are likely to be quite specific at this stage.

Post-inspection

During the post-inspection period the nursery/school receives further reports and has to be ready to respond to the team's findings. Shortly after the inspection the RI plus one or two of the team members will return to report back to the governors. They will not be quite so specific as they were with the headteacher and deputy headteacher, but they will highlight strengths and weaknesses, and present the governors with a list of areas that need to be addressed. A copy of the full written report will be forwarded a few weeks later. At this point the report becomes a public document and copies of it have to be available to parents. Once the inspection report has been received, there is a statutory requirement upon the governors to draw up an action plan to address those areas identified by the team as requiring change. Even if the governors disagree with an inspection finding they must institute action to bring about the change required in the final report.

Action plans identify

- clear targets and criteria for success;
- the action to be taken to meet the targets including strategies for monitoring and controlling the process;
- an indication of the timescales involved;
- possible funding or resourcing needed; and
- the member(s) of staff responsible.

Coping with an inspection as a class teacher

- Make sure the learning environment is attractive and stimulating for the children.
- Make sure your planning is available for the inspector to look at. Session planners should show clear and appropriate learning objectives.
- The quality of your teaching and the children's learning will be of prime concern to an inspector during an observation
  - Make sure you consider the different needs and abilities in your class. How are you going to differentiate for them?
  - Your questioning and exposition skills are important elements in ensuring that learning takes place. Have you thought through your questions, explanations and vocabulary?
  - The structure and organization of the lesson needs to be well thought out. Is there a clear beginning, middle and end? How are transition times going to be managed? Are your instructions clear? Is your timing and pacing suitable for the age and abilities of the children?
  - You need to maintain the children's interest and enthusiasm and keep them on task. This might be more difficult if you play it safe and plan a staid, completely risk-free lesson. How can you make your lesson interesting and exciting without losing control of events?

FURTHER SOURCES OF INFORMATION

The Responsibilities of the 3–8 Teacher

DfEE (1999) *Circular 12/99 School Teachers' Pay and Conditions of Employment 1999.* London: DfEE (www.dfee.gov.uk)

National Union of Teachers (1998) *1265 And All That.* London: NUT.

National Union of Teachers (1998) *Your Salary.* London: NUT.

School Teachers' Pay and Conditions Act 1991. London: HMSO.

Trend, R. (1997) *Qualified Teacher Status: A Practical Introduction.* London: Letts Educational.

Legislation Relating to Equality of Opportunity

Adams, J. (1994) '"She'll have a go at anything": Towards an Equal Opportunities Policy', in L. Abbot and R. Rodger (eds) *Quality Education in the Early Years*. Buckingham: Open University Press.

Commission for Racial Equality (www.cre.gov.uk)

Development Education Association (DEA), 29-31 Cowper Street, London, EC2A 4AP
(Tel. 020 7490 8123)

Equal Opportunities Commission (www.eoc.org.uk)

Race Relations Act 1976

Sex Discrimination Act 1975

Ensuring the Health and Safety of Young Children

Department of Education and Science (1989) *Curriculum Matters 13: Environmental Education from 5 to 16*. London: HMSO.

Health and Safety at Work Act 1974, Sections 7 and 8 (1974) London: HMSO.

National Curriculum Council (1990) *Environmental Education*. London: NCC.

Partington, J. (1984) *Law and the New Teacher*. London: Holt Education.

Children's Welfare

Children Act 1989: Section 3(5)

DfEE (1995) *Circular 10/95 Protecting Children from Abuse: The Role of the Education Service*. London: DfEE.

Kay, J. (1999) *Protecting Children: A Practical Guide*. London: Cassell.

Maintaining Good Order in the Classroom

DFE (1994) *Circular 8/94: Pupil Behaviour and Discipline*. London: DFE.

DFE (1994) *Circular 9/94 The Education of Children with Emotional and Behavioural Difficulties*. London: DFE and DoH.

DfEE (July, 1998) *Circular 10/98 Section 550A of the Education Act 1996: The Use of Force to Control or Restrain Pupils*. London: DfEE.

Robertson, J. (1989) *Effective Classroom Control*. London: Hodder and Stoughton.

Wragg, E. C. (1993) *Class Management*. London: Routledge.

Continuing Professional Development

DfEE (1990) 'Starting with Quality' (Report). London: DfEE

DfEE (1999) Induction Standards (www.dfee.gov.uk).

Maynard, T. (ed.) (1997) *An Introduction to Primary Mentoring*. London: Cassell.

Whole-school Approaches

Standards and Effectiveness Unit (1998) *A Scheme of Work for Key Stages 1 and 2: Geography*. London: QCA/DfEE.

Standards and Effectiveness Unit (1998) *A Scheme of Work for Key Stages 1 and 2: Information Technology*. London: QCA/DfEE.

Standards and Effectiveness Unit (1998) *A Scheme of Work for Key Stages 1 and 2: Design and Technology*. London: QCA/DfEE.

Working with Parents

Dean, J. (1993) *Organising Learning in the Primary School Classroom, 3rd edn*. London: Croom Helm.

Pollard, A. (1996) *An Introduction to Primary Education: For Parents, Governors and Student Teachers*. London: Cassell.

Strahan, H. (1997) '"You feel like you belong": establishing partnerships between parents and educators', in L. Abbott and R. Rodger (eds) *Quality Education in the Early Years*. Buckingham: Open University Press.

Managing Schools and Nurseries

DfEE (1998) *New Framework Governing Bodies: Circular 15/98*. London: DfEE.

Kenyon, P. (1998) *Ready for Inspection*. London: Scholastic.

Pollard, A. (1996) *An Introduction to Primary Education: For Parents, Governors and Student Teachers*. London: Cassell.

References

Abbott, L. (1994) 'The search for quality in the early years', in Abbott, L. and Rodger, R. (eds), *Quality Education in the Early Years*. Buckingham: Open University Press.

Adams, J. (1994) '"She'll have a go at anything": Towards an equal opportunities policy', in Abbott, L. and Rodger, R. (eds), *Quality Education in the Early Years*. Buckingham: Open University Press.

Alexander, R., Rose, J. and Woodhead, C. (1992) *Curriculum Organisation and Classroom Practice in Primary Schools: A Discussion Paper*. London: Department of Education and Science.

Athey, C. (1990) *Extending Thought in Young Children: A Parent–Teacher Partnership*. London: Chapman.

Barratt-Pugh, C. (1994) 'We only speak English here, don't we? Supporting language development in a multilingual context', in Abbott, L. and Rodger, R. (eds), *Quality Education in the Early Years*. Buckingham: Open University Press.

Bengtsson, J. (1995) 'What is reflection? On reflection in the teaching profession and teacher education', *Teachers and Teaching: Theory and Practice*, **1** (1) March, 23–32.

Bruce, T. (1997) *Early Childhood Education, 2nd edition*. London: Hodder and Stoughton.

Cotton, J. (1995) *The Theory of Learning: An Introduction*. London: Kogan Page.

Curry, M. and Bromfield, C. (1995) *Personal and Social Education for Primary Schools Through Circle Time*. Nasen Enterprises Ltd.

Davies, D. (1997) 'The relationship between science and technology in the primary curriculum: alternative perspectives', *The Journal of Design and Technology Education*, **2** (2) Summer, 101–11.

Dean, J. (1993) *Organising Learning in the Primary School Classroom, 3rd Edition*. London: Croom Helm.

Dearing, R. (1993) *The National Curriculum and its Assessment: Final Report*. London: School Curriculum and Assessment Authority.

DFE (1995a) Key Stages 1 and 2 of the National Curriculum. London: HMSO.

DFE (1990) '"Starting with Quality". Report of the Committee of Inquiry into the Quality of the Educational Experience offered to 3- and 4-year-olds', chaired by Mrs Angela Rumbold CBE, MP. Reprinted 1997.

DFE (1994) *Circular 9/94: The Education of Children with Emotional and Behavioural Difficlties*. London: DfE and DoH.

DfEE (1995b) *Circular 10/95: Protecting Children from Abuse: The Role of the Education Service*. London: DfEE.

DfEE (1998a) *Teaching: High Status, High Standards. Requirements for Courses of Initial Teacher Training*. London: Teacher Training Agency Publications.

DfEE (1998b) *Circular 10/98: The Use of Force to Control or Restrain Pupils*. London: DfEE.

DfEE (1998c) *Circular 15/98: New Framework Governing Bodies*. London: DfEE.

DfEE (1998d) *The National Literacy Strategy*. London: DfEE.

DfEE (1999a) *Induction Standards*. www.dfee.gov.uk.

DfEE (1999b) *Circular 12/99: School Teachers' Pay and Conditions of Employment 1999*. www.dfee.gov.uk.

DfEE (1999c) *The National Numeracy Strategy*. London: DfEE.

DES (1989) *Information Technology from 5 to 16: Curriculum Matters 15*. London: HMSO.

DES (1991) *The Teaching and Learning of Information Technology*. London: HMSO.

DES (1992) *The Education of Children Under Five*. London: HMSO.

Edwards, A. and Knight, P. (1994) *Effective Early Years Education: Teaching Young Children*. Buckingham: Open University Press.

Ellis, J. (1986) *Equal Opportunities and Computer Education in the Primary School*. Equal Opportunities Commission/ Microelectronics Education Support Unit.

Equal Opportunities Commission (1982) *Do You Provide Equal Opportunities?* Manchester: EOC.

Hughes, M. (1986) *Children and Number*. Oxford: Blackwell.

Kay, J. (1999) *Protecting Children: A Practical Guide*. London: Cassell.

Let's Get it Right (1996) Leeds City Council, Under Eights Service.

Megginson, S. (1990) *Developing Role Play*. Rotherham Metropolitan Borough Council, Department of Education.

NCC (1989) *A Curriculum for All: Special Needs in the National Curriculum*. York: NCC.

NCC (1990) *The Whole Curriculum*. York: NCC.

National Union of Teachers (1998a) *1265 And All That*. London: NUT.

National Union of Teachers (1998b) *Your Salary*. London: NUT.

Nottinghamshire County Council, Department of Education (1998) *Pupil Progress Record: Entry and Baseline Assessment*. Nottinghamshire County Council.

Osborne, R. and Freyberg, P. (eds) (1985) *Learning in Science: The Implications of Children's Science*. London: Heinemann.

QCA (1998a) *Maintaining Breadth and Balance at Key Stages 1 and 2*. London: QCA Publications.

QCA (1998b) *Early Years Conference Report* (www.qca.org)

QCA (1999a) *Review of Desirable Learning Outcomes: Consultation Report*. London: QCA Publications.

QCA (1999b) *Keeping Track: Effective Ways of Recording Pupil Achievement to Help Raise Standards*. London: QCA Publications.

QCA (1999e) *Investing in Our Future: Early Learning Goals*. London: QCA.

Roberts, T. (1983) *Child Management in the Primary School*. London: Unwin.

Robertson, J. (1989) *Effective Classroom Control*. London: Hodder and Stoughton.

SCAA (1994) *Evaluation of the Implementation of Science in the National Curriculum at Key Stages 1, 2 and 3. Vol. 3: Differentiation*. London: SCAA.

SCAA (1995) *Planning the Curriculum at Key Stages 1 and 2*. London: SCAA.

SCAA (1996) *Nursery Education: Desirable Outcomes for Children's Learning on Entering Compulsory Education*. London: DfEE/SCAA.

SCAA (1997) *Looking at Children's Learning*. London: SCAA.

School Examination and Assessment Council (1991) *Children's Work Assessed: Key Stage 1*. London: HMSO.

Selley, N. (1999) *The Art of Constructivist Teaching in the Primary School: A Guide to Students and Teachers*. London: David Fulton Publishers.

Sharman, C., Cross, W. and Vennis, D. (1998) *Observing Children: A Practical Guide*. London: Cassell.

Stradling, B. and Saunders, L. (1993) 'Differentiation in practice: responding to the needs of all pupils', *Educational Research*, **35** (2) Summer, pp. 127–37.

Task Group on Assessment and Testing (1987) *A Report*. London: DES.

Waterhouse, P. (1983) *Managing the Learning Process*. New York: McGraw-Hill.

Wragg, E. C. (1993) *Class Management*. London: Routledge.

Index